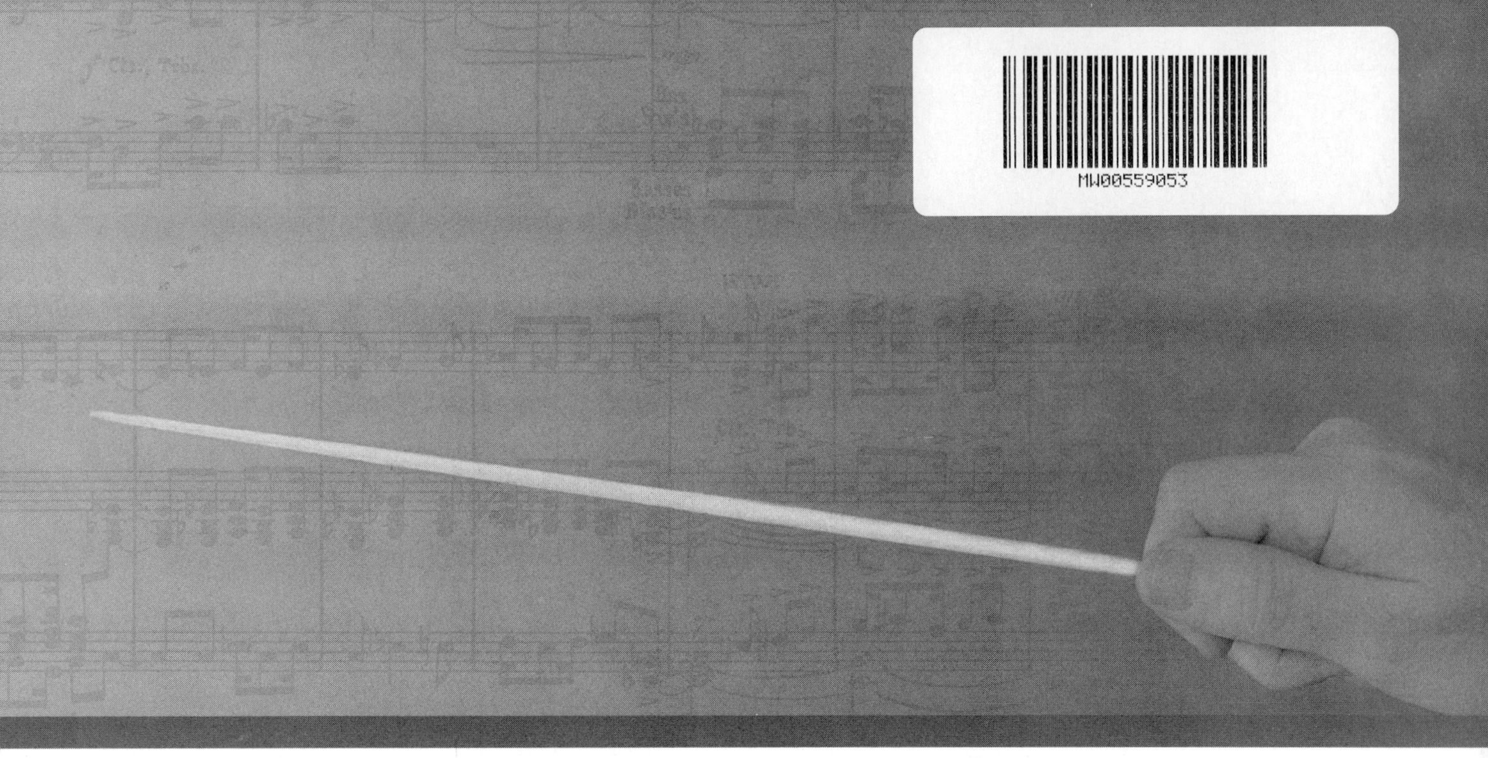

Conducting

The Art of Communication

Wayne Bailey
Arizona State University

New York Oxford
OXFORD UNIVERSITY PRESS
2009

Oxford University Press, Inc., publishes works that further Oxford University's objective of excellence in research, scholarship, and education.

Oxford New York
Auckland Cape Town Dar es Salaam Hong Kong Karachi
Kuala Lumpur Madrid Melbourne Mexico City Nairobi
New Delhi Shanghai Taipei Toronto

With offices in
Argentina Austria Brazil Chile Czech Republic France Greece
Guatemala Hungary Italy Japan Poland Portugal Singapore
South Korea Switzerland Thailand Turkey Ukraine Vietnam

Published by Oxford University Press, Inc.
198 Madison Avenue, New York, New York 10016
http://www.oup.com

Library of Congress Cataloging-in-Publication Data

Bailey, Wayne, 1955–
Conducting: the art of communication / Wayne Bailey.
p. cm.
Includes bibliographical references (p.) and index.
ISBN 978-0-19-536651-8 (spiral (main)) 1. Conducting. I. Title
MT85.B143 2009
781.45—dc22
2007038721

Printing number: 9 8 7 6 5 4 3 2 1

Printed in the United States of America
on acid-free paper

Contents

Preface

Conducting is one of the most demanding and enjoyable of the musical arts. To be a successful conductor one must simultaneously be a musician, juggler, psychologist, historian, theorist, and cheerleader. Like other musicians, the conductor spends many hours alone in a room preparing, but unlike other musical artists, the conductor rarely gets to practice with his or her instrument. This problem extends into the curricula of most music schools, where students might spend years studying music theory and then be expected to learn how to conduct in fifteen weeks. Conducting courses have become "synthesis" classes where undergraduates must, finally, put together all the parts of knowledge and skill they have learned in other classes. Over the years music faculty have changed the curriculum of conducting class from a skills-based course to a class where students learn to put into practice all the musicianship and psychology training they have amassed in three or four years of college. The study of conducting is now a required part of nearly every undergraduate curriculum in music schools.

Many books have been written to address the topic—some focusing on conducting as an art, many taking a strictly pedagogical standpoint, and a few of a historical nature. At some time in their careers, almost all musicians take up the baton to conduct for some reason or other, either as a full-time position or often for some specific event or performance. There have been a few popular or successful conducting textbooks aimed at teaching the art of conducting, but none satisfactorily address the technical, analytical, and expressive aspects of conducting.

This text is designed to guide the student to becoming an artist who leads colleagues in the re-creation of the music as the composer intended.

AUDIENCE

Over the years, as an administrator and reviewer of music schools, I've seen that colleges and universities offer conducting classes in many different ways. Most music schools require different numbers of conducting classes based upon the objectives of the degree programs. Students in some degree programs, such as guitar performance or music therapy, for example, need acquire only the rudimentary techniques and understanding of conducting. Other programs, such as music education, require more advanced skills in expressive conducting, score analysis, and error detection. I've written this text to accommodate those different requirements; there is enough material here to allow the book to be used in a two-semester sequence in conducting, but it may also be used in one-semester instrumental conducting courses.

There is no other text designed to work in a two-semester conducting sequence. Almost any of the leading texts would be sufficient for an introductory, technique-only, one-semester course in conducting, but none are very usable in an advanced course. Rather than have two different books for a two-semester course sequence or, more commonly, no textbook for the second course, instructors may find this text more useful.

ORGANIZATION

The book emphasizes the whole conductor, not just his or her baton technique. Most conducting texts spend an inordinate amount of time on simple conducting pattern development with elaborate drawings of 4/4, 3/4, 2/4, etc. patterns. While this is an important aspect of any conducting course, this material only takes two or three class meetings to teach. This text includes this material and also includes sections on artistic and expressive development, as well as the development of the conductor's ear. The text is divided into four topics: basic techniques, advanced techniques (including expression), score preparation, and error detection. The instructor can choose topics from some or all of the units based upon the goals of the student or the specific course. The text contains material focusing on technical conducting skills, expressive conducting, score preparation, and error detection. Some of the units assume that the student already has experience in music theory, music history, and some knowledge of the instruments.

FEATURES

Most conducting texts focus primarily on right- and left-hand/arm technique. This book gives instruction in technique but focuses as much on the use of other expressive aspects of conducting like facial expression and body movement. Also, more instruction time is devoted to the use of the hands and arms in expressive movement than in many other conducting textbooks.

Score analysis and preparation is one of the most important tasks of a conductor. This aspect of conducting is completely ignored in almost all conducting texts. This text offers a method for analysis and preparation as well as sample analyses of two standard works from the repertory. It emphasizes this aspect of conducting to an equal extent as the technical skills required and impresses upon the student that conducting gestures must relate to the conductor's knowledge of the score.

Conductors also spend a good deal of time recognizing and correcting errors. Yet few books and courses provide students with instruction in this important skill. University courses in ear training or sight singing seem to do a poor job of preparing students for this type of aural skill. This text contains information on error recognition and correction as well as exercises for use in class that provide practice in error detection.

EXERCISES

I've carefully chosen a unique set of exercises to illustrate specific technical and expressive problems in conducting. They are purposefully short. Most conducting classes have up to twenty students in each section. While this provides a nice-sized ensemble for the conductors to work with, it also means that the students' podium time will be very limited. The exercises in this text go directly to the conducting problem with little time spent leading up to the issue. They are, for the most part, arrangements of great works of the standard literature of the band, choir, and orchestra from the Baroque era to modern times. These exercises are aimed at both technique and artistry, not just one or the other. They are not aimed at the teaching of music literature, but students do become familiar with the primary themes of great musical works by preparing the exercises.

ANCILLARY MATERIALS

One of the most frustrating problems facing conducting teachers is finding exercises that work with the instrumentation of each individual class. To help solve this problem, we've created a CD-ROM of the Finale files of each conducting exercise in the book, which is available free of charge to adopting instructors. This allows the instructor to make custom orchestrations to fit a specific class. Doing so provides the student with a more score-like experience than does conducting from the four-part concert pitch versions of the exercises printed in the text; the exercises thus become much more musical in nature, which in turn helps the student conductor learn to be a more expressive conductor. From the Finale files the instructor might also create MP3 files for the students to use in their individual practice.

ACKNOWLEDGMENTS

In any endeavor as large as writing a textbook, there are many people to thank. I am grateful to Jan Beatty, Executive Editor, Cory Schneider, Assistant Editor, and Barbara Mathieu, Production Editor, at Oxford University Press for their assistance with the text and belief that the world might need just one more textbook on conducting. The assistance of conductors who have reviewed and tested the book at universities across the nation has been most helpful, including: Terry Austin, Virginia Commonwealth University; Douglas Bianchi, Wayne State University; Robert Glassman, Wichita State University; Christopher Knighten, East Carolina University; Joseph Missal, Oklahoma State University; Tom O'Neal, University of Missouri–Columbia; Eric Rombach-Kendall, University of New Mexico; Thomas Verrier, Vanderbilt University; and John M. Watkins, Jr., University of Florida. The graduate conducting students at Arizona State University who tested the book include James Smart, Andy Collinsworth, and Matthew Luttrel and their efforts and ideas have proved invaluable to the final version of the text. And, of course, the students in conducting classes at Arizona State University have greatly contributed to the final text. I am grateful to the administration of the School of Music at Arizona State University, including J. Robert Wills, former Dean of the Herberger College of Fine Arts; Kwang-Wu Kim, Dean of the Herberger College of Arts; and Kimberly Marshall, Director of the School of Music. My instrumental conducting colleagues at ASU, Gary Hill and Timothy Russell, daily inspire me to be a better conductor. Finally, I am forever indebted to Joseph Christensen and Allan McMurray for helping me communicate with my ensembles rather than merely conduct them.

UNIT

1

Introduction *to the* Art *of* Conducting

CHAPTER 1

The Art of Conducting

PURPOSE AND TRAINING OF CONDUCTORS

Why do we need conductors? Today's musicians think of one musician standing in front of them telling them how, when, and what to play as completely normal. However, when one considers the entire history of music, the conductor of today is a relatively new member of the musical ensemble. How did conducting develop and why did it need to? This is a question that conductors should understand if they are to develop their technical, musical, and leadership skills to a high enough level to lead their colleagues.

Generally speaking, we have conductors when we need them. If a group is small enough, or the music is simple enough, a conductor is not used. Chamber music very rarely uses a conductor. It is only when some aspect of the music is too complex to perform without a visual aid of some kind, or when an ensemble is so large that the group benefits from one person's interpretive leadership, that we call upon conductors.

The conductor exists for at least the following purposes:

- To represent the composer.
- To serve as the musical leader of the ensemble.
- To make and carry out certain administrative decisions.
- To inspire and control the ensemble.

Serving as the musical leader of the ensemble carries some heavy responsibilities. It means that the conductor's vision and interpretation of the music will be the most important of any of the musicians in the ensemble. The conductor must provide an informed interpretation of the music through his own knowledge of musical style and performance practice, compositional style of the composer, and historical aspects of the work and composer. He must have an analytical understanding of the work to be conducted that provides an interpretation of phrase structures, climaxes, tempo markings, and dynamic, articulation, and ornamental markings. The ability to understand a composition from a musical sense is more important than the development of excellent stick technique. In short, the conductor must be the best-informed musician in the ensemble. The conductor brings to the ensemble the primary interpretation of the work to be performed.

The aspiring conductor first must become the best musician possible on one instrument. This intensive study of a primary instrument mirrors that of the performance student who plans to spend his career performing. The depth of musicianship acquired by the conductor on his instrument relates directly to the depth of musical understanding he possesses as a conductor.

The modern conductor is open to ideas of the other excellent musicians in the ensemble, but in the end it is he who must make the final interpretative musical decisions so that the ensemble can perform the work in a cohesive fashion.

The conductor is also an administrator. This is true to some degree whether one is conducting the finest orchestra in the world or the most inexperienced beginning-level elementary band. It is the conductor that sets the order of the rehearsal, decides the set-up and chair placement of the ensemble, and sets the tone and mood of the rehearsal. In all cases except with union ensembles, the conductor decides when to begin, when to take breaks, and when the rehearsal is finished. Ensemble members readily accept and expect this of a conductor, knowing that such an arrangement saves time and creates an ordered environment in which they can make music.

The conductor must have the ability to control and inspire large groups of people, especially in the rehearsal setting. This also includes the ability and willingness to criticize and correct the playing of individuals. This error detection and correction is one of the most important things that a conductor does in rehearsal. He must also learn to accurately detect errors, point them out to the performer using a positive demeanor, and, if necessary, make technical and musical suggestions to the performer as to how to correct the problem. Controlling the ensemble simply means keeping the performers on task, eliminating unnecessary conversation, and pacing the rehearsal so that it is an efficient use of time. The conductor must be knowledgeable in the areas of psychology and group dynamics. He must possess a force of will and demeanor capable of inspiring others to follow his commands and suggestions and to accept his criticisms.

Inspiring people is a difficult and delicate matter. The musicians must have confidence in the conductor's ability both as a musician and as a conductor. The ensemble members look to the conductor to be an excellent musician who deals with them in an efficient and caring manner, but who also has high musical expectations for the group.

The conductor must also be the composer's advocate. He must accurately represent the composer's intent through the interpretation and performance of the work. Knowledge of the composer's style and conductor analysis of the work is essential to assist the ensemble in achieving a representative performance of the work.

The training of conductors is woefully informal in music schools. In most cases conductors learn their craft on the job. In some manner this is necessary, since, unlike learning our individual instruments, we cannot take an ensemble with us three or four hours each day to a practice room while we are in school. However, conductors can prepare themselves musically even if they cannot gain much actual practical experience with an ensemble.

Finally, a conductor must possess a breadth of life experience. As Bruno Walter said, "One who is no more than a musician, is half a musician."[1] Conductors must study art, literature, and theater and experience life itself in order to bring depth of understanding to the scores they conduct.

DEVELOPMENT OF CONDUCTING

As stated above, conducting developed over the centuries because of a need. As Western art music became more complex and ensembles became larger and mixed with voices, communication between the musicians became more difficult.

The first musical leaders were members of the ensembles that they led. In fact, until the mid-1800s the typical conductor was often a keyboard player and/or composer in the group. Prior to that time, to have a musician in the ensemble who did nothing but conduct would have been very unusual. From the beginning, conductors were administrators as well as musical leaders. Especially in sacred music performances of the Middle Ages, Renaissance, and Baroque periods, the conductor was usually a senior ensemble member who played various instruments, taught music at the church, composed music for the services, led his musician colleagues in performance, and handled all the administration of the music program as well. Conductors in secular music were rare. Instead, most often the leader of secular music was someone who owned instruments and/or music and served as the administrator of the group. In these cases the leader was often not the finest musician of the ensemble.

Much has been written about the early development of hand signs to indicate musical cues to ensembles members. In many situations musical leaders carried a staff, a stick of some kind, or rolled up paper to help them indicate the beat when necessary. Out of necessity, musical leaders combined hand signals and the rhythmic beating of something with administrative/leadership abilities to make up the primitive shape of today's conductor.

The development of the score also contributed to the establishment of the need for a conductor. Scores as we know them today were not used in ensembles regularly until the Classical period, and then not if the work was conducted by the composer. Early ensemble leaders had to study each part separately and form the overall idea of the work in their heads. This worked until some time in the Baroque era, when the size of ensembles and the length of works made this impractical, at least for rehearsal purposes. Especially because of the advent of opera in the early Baroque period, it became necessary for the musical leader to work from a score of some fashion that included all the parts.

The combination of all these elements—tradition of hand signs, use of some form of staff or baton, use of a score to rehearse—led to the establishment of the importance of having a conductor lead a group. After the mid-1800s the modern-day conductor became common. However, our concept of the conductor as the primary musician of the ensemble, someone who is famous in his own right as a musician, did not develop until the very late 1800's. Until then conductors were often obscure figures, not listed on programs, and often subservient to the star singer or instrumentalist. The idea of a conductor as famous as Michael Tilson Thomas, Kurt Masur, or Lorin Mazel is a product of the twentieth century. The complexities of works by composers such as Richard Wagner cemented the place of the conductor, and Wagner's primary conductor Hans von Bülow was the first true conductor as we think of them today. Not a composer, nor a great virtuoso on any instrument, von Bülow became famous and important for his abilities to lead and inspire musicians to interpretive accuracy of some of the most difficult music of his age. Many of the twentieth century's greatest conductors were also composers and virtuosi—Leonard Bernstein and Daniel Barenboim leap to mind. However, the conductor today is first a musician and conductor, and second a composer and/or virtuoso. This is exactly the opposite of our predecessors from the Baroque and Classical eras.

NOTE

1. Walter, Bruno. *Of Music and Music Making*. W.W. Norton, New York, 1961.

CHAPTER 2

The Language of Conducting

Like any area of study, conducting has its own unique terms and commonly used phrases employed to describe aspects of the art. In order for musicians to communicate effectively, they must share a common language. Terms included and described in this chapter are the fundamental words we assign to gestures of conducting.

ICTUS

An ictus is more of a place than a thing. The point in a standard beat pattern where the stick changes direction and the primary beat or pulse occurs is the ictus. An ictus can be anywhere in the field of conducting that the conductor places it. The standard beat patterns that have developed over the years are created by repeatedly placing each ictus of the pattern at approximately the same point each time the pattern is repeated.

REBOUND

The rebound is created by changing the direction of the stick away from the ictus point. It might be best to think of this as an action as well as a thing. The size and style of rebound will show the ensemble members the style of the music and will probably be determined by the speed and style of the music itself.

PREPARATORY BEAT

Usually abbreviated to the shorter "prep beat," this, like rebound, is both an action and a thing. The prep beat(s) (sometimes there are multiples) is the "impulse of will" gesture that causes an ensemble to produce a sound. The prep beat should indicate when to start the tone (ictus point) and the tempo, dynamic, style, and articulation of the sound that the conductor wishes the ensemble to produce. The prep beat is the most important conducting gesture that the conductor gives to the ensemble.

ACTIVE/PASSIVE GESTURES

Not all conducting gestures are created equal. The conductor must be able to vary the appearance of gestures in order to give context to the performer; otherwise, all gestures would garner the same effect. An active gesture is one that the conductor expects to produce a sound.

The passive gesture is one that gives information, but should not create a sound response from the performer. The combination and alternation of both active and passive gestures gives the performer the proper scope to interpret the meaning of the conductor's gestures.

HINGES

Hinges are the joints or parts of the body used to create gestures and include the shoulder, the elbow, the wrist, and the fingers as primary hinges. Most conductors also sometimes use the neck, the waist, and the knees (not recommended often) as secondary hinge points. The more hinges employed in any gesture, the more lyrical or fluid the gesture. Staccato or marcato conducting gestures employ fewer hinges than do legato gestures.

RELEASES

A release is the ending of a note. It can be abrupt, or it can decay, or crescendo. Release in conducting usually refers to notes that are followed by silence—either a rest or by the end of the work. A release requires different conducting gestures that match the type of sound desired. Actual physical gestures for releases are discussed in Chapter 4.

CUES

A cue is a visual aid of some kind that is not pulse/beat related and is intended to aid the performer in the execution of a part. Often a cue is used to aid the performer upon first entrance, or after a long series of measures of rests. The cue can be given by either hand, or sometimes with the head and/or eyes. Development of cues is covered in Chapter 5.

GESTURE OF SYNCOPATION

The gesture of syncopation is the movement made by a conductor that causes a player to perform a sound on an off-beat, or portion of a beat. It is often an accented, or abrupt movement, and it must occur on the pulse immediately preceding the entrance.

MIRROR CONDUCTING

When both hands are moving in unison gesture, the conductor is said to be "mirror" conducting.

TRAVEL

Travel is the distance between two ictus points.

CHAPTER 3

Podium Posture

Appropriate stance and posture on the podium are important aspects of conducting. It is essential that the conductor convey the general style of the music being performed through body carriage, body movement, facial expressions, and general conducting skills. A natural, yet commanding posture is required to be an effective leader from the podium. Posture and stance communicate energy to the ensemble. The energy level of the music determines the energy contained within the posture of the conductor.

STANCE

The conductor should be erect with head up, a straight back, shoulders relaxed and back, but not high. The chest should be forward, not collapsed. Feet should be placed in a modified ballet position with the right heel in the in step of the left foot. Once conducting has begun, the conductor is encouraged to step away from this seemingly rigid position, but still maintaining the basic posture described. The weight should be balanced equally on both feet. Excessive movement or dancing on the podium is to be discouraged, since it is a distraction from the music for both performers and audience. The beginning conductor might try conducting on a small podium to keep from moving to the left and right too much.

Common problems with stance include slumped shoulders and feet too widely spread apart. Both of these stance problems create arm control and movement problems and should be avoided.

POSITION OF ARMS AND HANDS

The best position of the hands and arms can be described as a rounded extension of the arms with bent elbows. To achieve the correct position, extend the arms straight out in front of you such that they are perpendicular to the ground with

Example 3.1
Conducting stance.

palms down and a shoulder width apart. Next, allow your elbows to bend slightly, with your hands drawing towards your body. It is important to not lower the arms when bending the elbows. When at the conducting position, the tip of the baton should be high enough to be between the conductor's eyes and the performer's eyes. This allows the performer to see the conductor's face and the baton simultaneously, without having to choose between the two.

The conductor should think of reaching out to the ensemble—not with stiff arms, but also not allowing the elbows to completely bend and relax. The baton tip should point slightly to the conductor's left and should look like an extension of the arm. This conducting position is often referred to as "hugging the barrel" because when executed, the arms create a rounded space in front of the conductor. The conductor should not fully extend the arms toward the ensemble into a sort of "superman" position. Not only does this look odd, but it takes away the flexibility of the hinges along the arm.

Example 3.2 Conducting position.

The primary conducting gesture is a combination of the elbow and shoulder hinges. Allowing the plane to drop low causes conductors to use their elbows as their primary hinge; the arms are collapsed towards the conductor such that the pattern is produced by the elbow movement alone. This position, although feeling relaxed, is not conducive to expressive conducting.

The left hand should be held in a graceful position—one that is neither tense nor completely limp. You will notice that once in this position, the left hand is generally pointing at the baton. You should not actually point at the baton, but the left hand should direct attention to the baton hand. The fingers of the left hand should be together but look relaxed. The shape of the hand should convey the idea of motion and should complement rather than contrast with the baton and grip.

Posture can also be used to cause the ensemble, to create different sounds. If a conductor steps or leans toward the ensemble, the players will generally increase the intensity of their sounds and/or get louder. The opposite is also true; as the conductor leans back, the ensemble tends to relax and play lighter. A similar effect is achieved by using one's full height. As the posture is more upright and tall, the ensemble responds with a formal, often accented sound. As the conductor relaxes and allow the body to shrink, the players allow their sounds to become less intense, and often softer.

PARTS OF THE BATON

Batons come in a variety of lengths and have many differently shaped handles. Both the length and the shape of the handle (or ball/heel) can affect a conductor's style and ability to communicate with the ensemble effectively.

Example 3.3
Baton heel shapes.

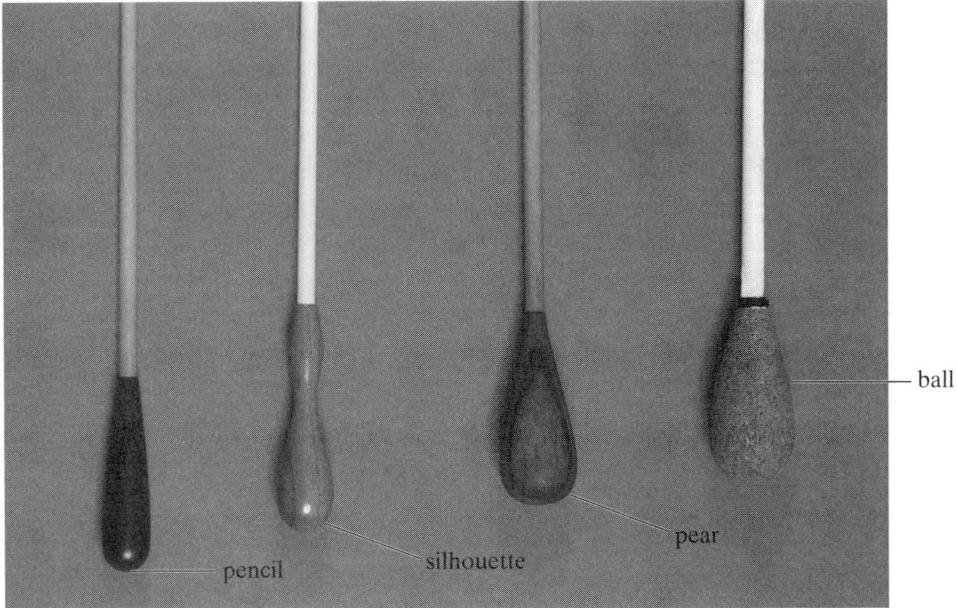

There are four primary parts of the baton: tip, shaft, balance point, and ball/heel. The ball/heel is the largest part of the baton and is used to hold the baton. This part of the baton is usually round, pear shaped, or a cylindrical. The shape of the ball/heel is a matter of preference: the shape that feels most comfortable in the hand is the one that should be used.

The shaft is the long narrow section of the baton that ends with the tip. The length of the shaft should be in proportion to the conductor's arm and the size of the ensemble. Generally, the most comfortable length of baton is the same as the distance from the center of the palm to the crook of the elbow. The larger the ensemble, the larger the baton.

The balance point is the point along the shaft at which the baton's weight can be evenly balanced. This balance point can be altered by adding a weight in the heel of the baton.

Batons are usually made of wood or fiberglass. The best batons are wooden because they have the least flexibility. Fiberglass batons tend to have much flexibility at the tip, which can cause lack of clarity on the ictus. Many batons are now made of graphite, which is more durable and lighter than wood.

Example 3.4
Baton parts.

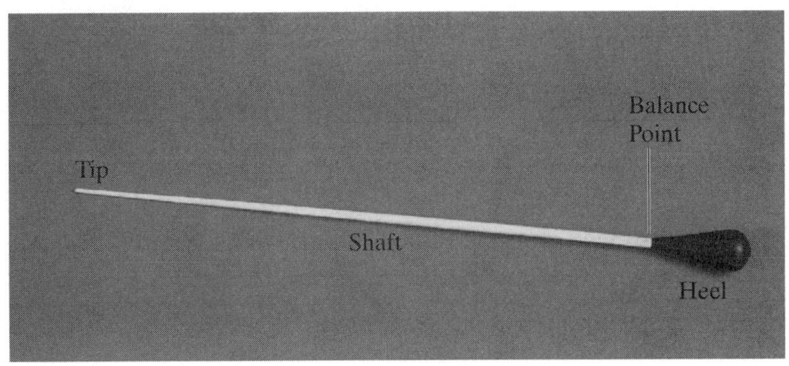

HOLDING THE BATON

The baton should always be held in the right hand.

The grip of the baton can be properly achieved in five easy steps. First, extend the right hand as if ready to shake hands, keeping the fingers and thumb together. Second, turn the hand so that the palm is facing up. Next, lay the baton across the palm at an angle with the ball/handle resting in the palm. Fourth, lightly roll the fingers around the ball/handle. Finally, turn the hand back over so that the palm is facing down. The baton should primarily be controlled by the thumb and index finger. The palm of the hand serves as an anchor point for the heel of the baton. The baton should look like a natural extension of the arm as it is held in the hand.

Step 1

Step 2

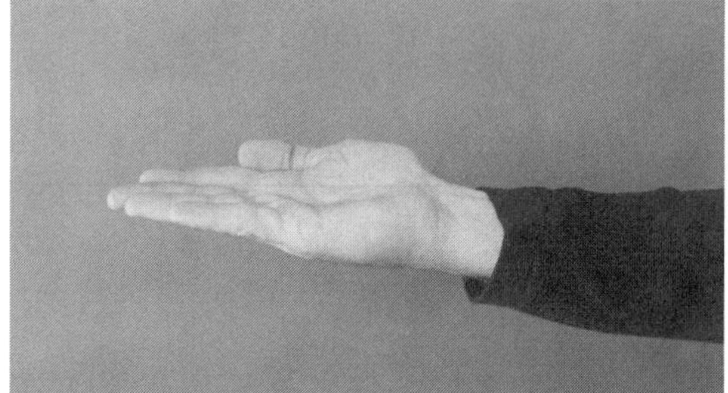

Step 3

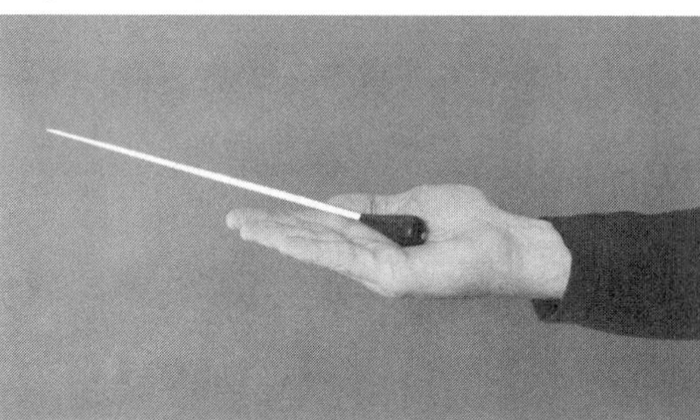

Step 4

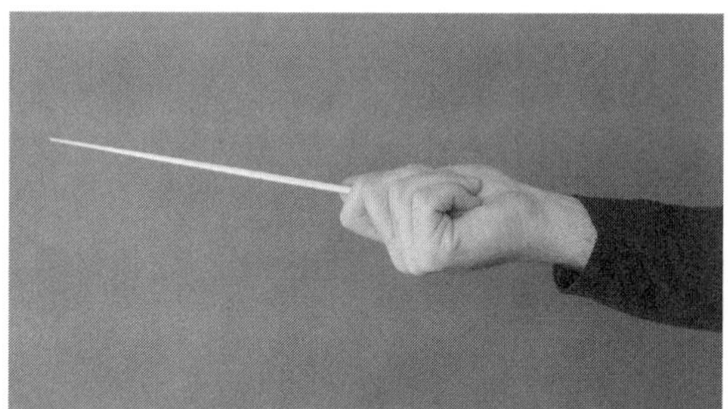

Step 5

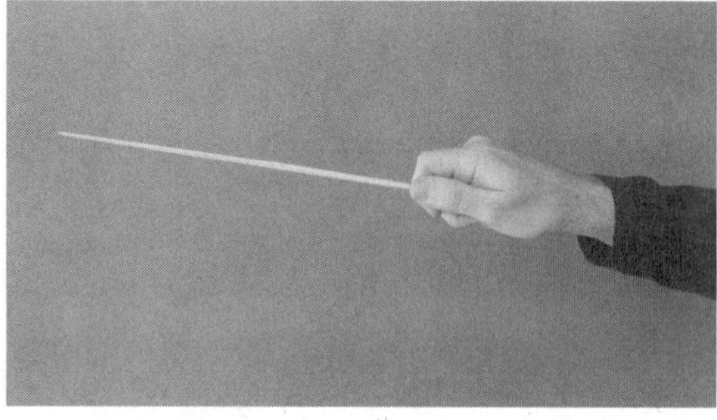

Example 3.5 Baton grip.

Index finger on top of baton

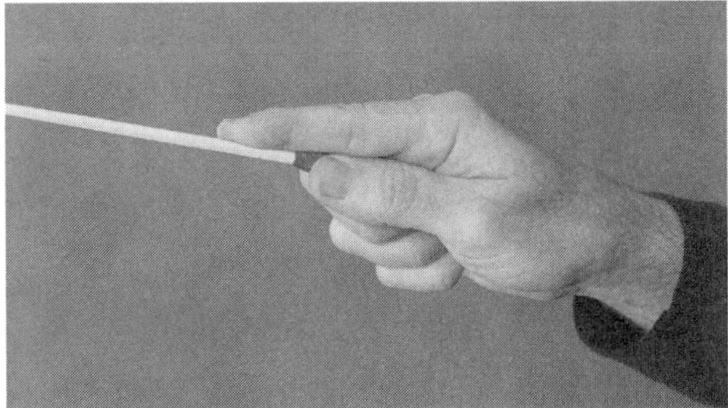

Flying fingers

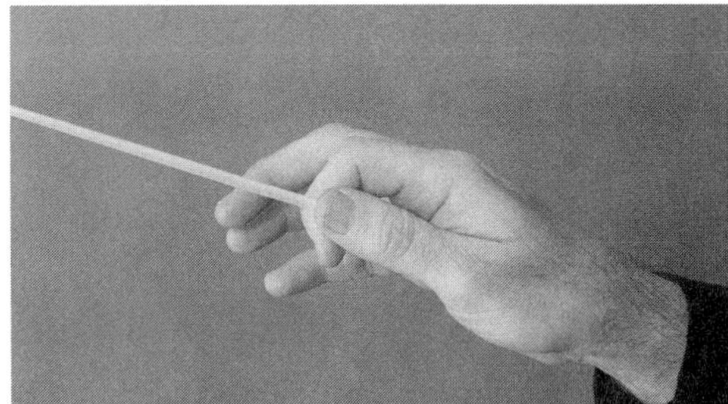

Baton held by ball

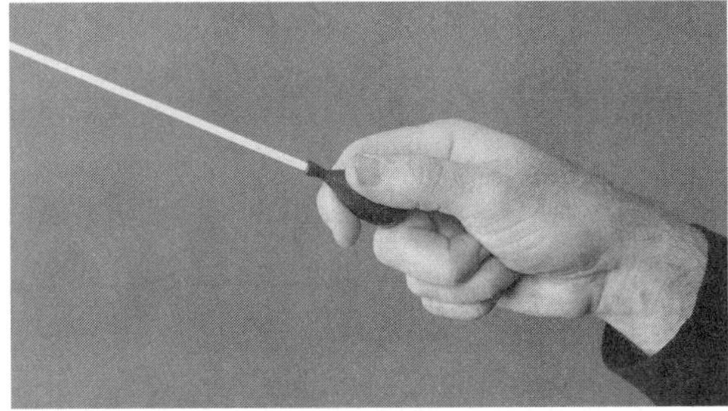

Grip too tight

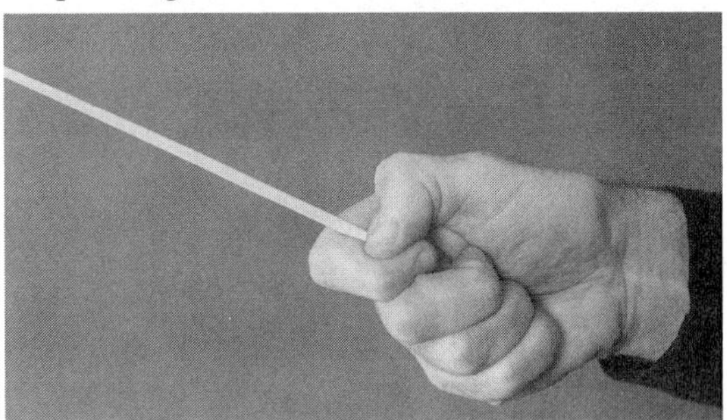

Example 3.6 Incorrect baton grips.

The conductor should avoid placing the index finger on top of the baton because this eliminates one of the expressive hinges. Wrapping the fingers loosely around the baton eliminates "flying fingers" and other distracting openhanded grips. The conductor should also avoid holding the heel/ball of the baton between the fingers as this creates an insecure and loose grip. Any grip that allows the tip of the baton to point up or down should be discouraged. The grip should create the illusion of the baton being an extension of the arm.

THE READY POSITION

It is effective for the conductor to fashion his own "ready" position to be used to help start the ensemble. This signals to the ensemble that the music is about to begin and gathers the attention of all the players. The following steps are suggested as an example that has proved effective.

1. Step onto the podium (You should do most talking and administrative business off the podium. The podium is for music making.) and assume the stance suggested above.
2. Bring your arms up to the ready conducting position to establish your conducting plane, but keep them about three feet apart.
3. Bring your hands in together to the ready conducting position (left hand about the same height as the right and gently curved toward the baton). This move is the "gathering gesture," and it will prove very effective in focusing the player's attention to the baton and your eyes.

GESTURE BOX

The primary gestures of both hands of the conductor should take place within a "conducting gesture box." This box contains the pattern and icti of the patterns. The placement of the center of this box determines the "conducting plane." The plane is an imaginary horizontal line on which the downbeat ictus occurs. It is important that the center of the box be high enough such that the baton tip is between the eyes of the performers and the conductor's baton tip and eyes. Note here that this does not mean placing the hands between the conductor and ensemble eyes—this would block the eyes. Having the tip of the baton at eye level actually allows the hands to be lower.

The gesture box is a series of concentrically centered boxes that change size according to the dynamic range of the music. The largest gesture box for any conductor is the vertical space from the top of his head to the waist and the reach of the arms horizontally. The size of the gestures is determined by a number of things, including the style of the music and the number of players in the ensemble. For example, it takes a smaller gesture to gain a forte sound out of eight players than

Example 3.7
Gesture box.

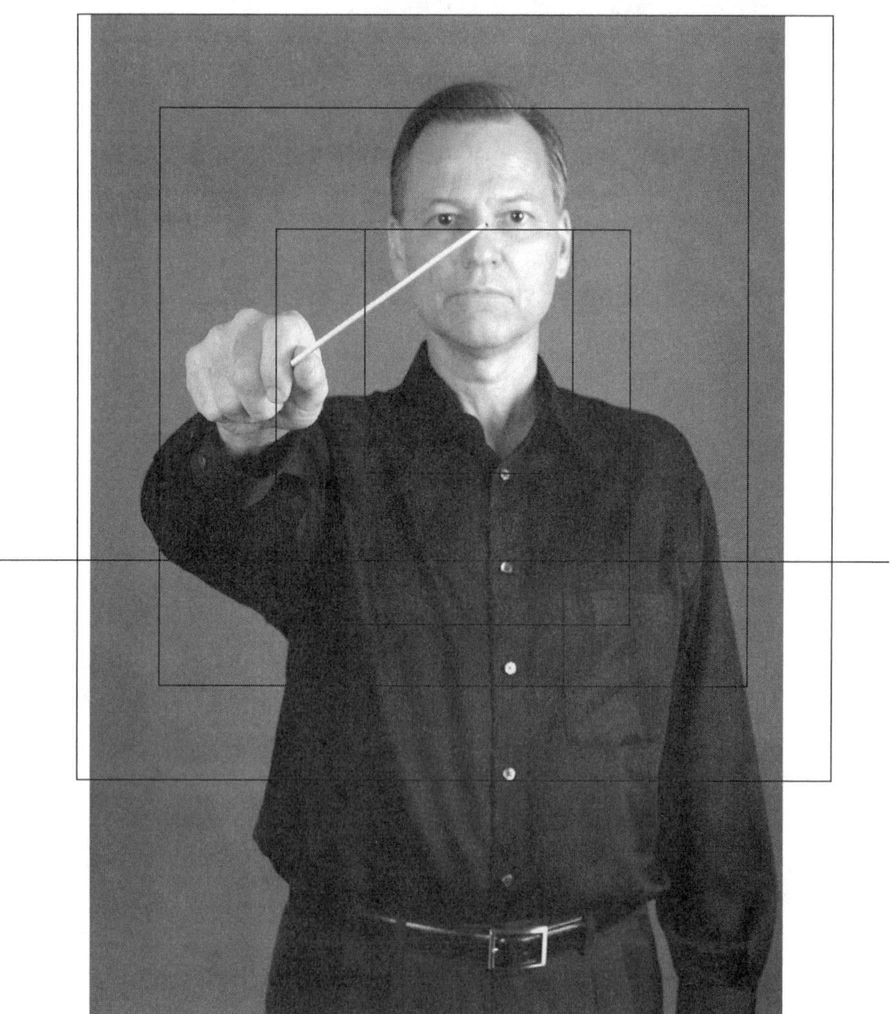

from eighty. The center of the box must not change its vertical position. The conducting plane should remain high and not slip so low that it appears that the tip of the baton is at chin level. The baton tip must remain at eye level.

The most common gesture box problem among beginning conductors is having the centerpoint too low. This creates a low plane of conducting, which forces the ensemble members to choose between looking at the conductor's eyes or the baton. A low centerpoint also allows the conductor to collapse the elbows backwards. While this might feel better initially than keeping the arms higher, it also limits the number of hinges that can be used to express the music, specifically the shoulder hinge.

The conductor's gesture box and centerpoint move along with the eyes and baton. If the music requires that the conductor address patterns to the right or left sides of the ensemble, he must use the waist hinge to pivot rather than turning the feet. Keeping the lower body pointing toward the center of the ensemble and pivoting the upper body allows for fluid and easy movement left to right as needed.

The gesture box also extends toward and away from the ensemble, not just left/right and up/down. This gives the gestures another dimensional plane (see Chapter 6). At this point it is enough for the conductor to realize that the hands must be placed at a different place in this plane. If the conductor wants the baton hand to be the focus of the players, then that hand must be closer to the ensemble. If the left hand's gestures are more important, then the left hand must be placed closer to the players.

CHAPTER 4

Basic Pattern Development

The development of basic conducting patterns is the first step toward becoming a proficient conductor. The patterns serve as the building blocks with which conductors and ensembles communicate. The fluid and easy production of these patterns must become as natural to the conductor as walking and talking. Without this developed ease the conductor is forced to focus too much energy on patterns, to the detriment of critical listening and expressive conducting. While easy and natural pattern production is a requirement for excellent conducting, it is only the first step in the conductor's development.

PREPARATORY GESTURES

The preparatory beat is the most important movement that the conductor gives to the ensemble. When performed correctly it tells the ensemble when to play, how fast to play, what dynamic to play, and in what style to play. This is a great amount of information to pack into one or sometimes two prep beats, and the conducting student should pay a good deal of time and attention to practicing these gestures.

The prep beat is most often an upward movement. This is because much music begins on count 1. In any case the prep beat for an on-beat entrance should be the ictus of the beat that precedes the first musical sound. For example, if a work begins on count 4, the prep beat given should be in the general direction of count 3. If the work begins on count 1, the prep beat should be an upward motion since beat 1 is always a downward motion.

If a work begins on an"off-beat, the conductor must give at least two preparatory beats; this gesture is discussed in a later chapter.

The first step to a good prep beat is to direct the focus of the ensemble to the podium. This can be best achieved by assuming the correct stance, raising your arms to the conducting position in a rounded and "gathering" fluid gesture. Finally, make eye contact with the performers once you are in the ready position.

Example 4.1
Preparatory beat.

Many conductors believe that the intake of a breath simultaneously with the preparatory beat aids the players in the initial sound. If the conductor chooses to do this, the breath should not be an audible gasp but should be a normal breath in style with the music to be performed.

The size of the prep beat given will indicate to the ensemble the basic dynamic volume required. This is also aided by use or lack of movement of the body. The larger the prep beat, the louder the expected volume of the ensemble response.

The conductor's posture and facial expression generally convey the mood or style of the work, and the prep beat must match that style. If the music is of a legato nature, the prep beat must be a smooth, fluid gesture. When the style of music is marcato or staccato, the conductor must give a prep beat in a more accented style.

The speed of the prep beat tells the ensemble the basic tempo of the work. Many experienced conductors believe that tempo cannot be indicated with just one prep beat and therefore give two or more. In this case one of the prep beats must be more active than the others or the ensemble will become confused. The passive prep beat will lack the "gesture of intent" and will indicate tempo only.

The ictus of the preparatory beat must be on the same plane as the ictus of the first sound. To place either in another place confuses the ensemble because the preparatory ictus implies that this will be the point of return for the start of the sounded beat.

PATTERNS

Over the centuries conducting beat patterns have become standardized. The pattern will look different when diagrammed based upon the style of the music. The first (left-hand) diagram shows how the pattern will look to the ensemble when the music is of a lyrical nature and the second (right-hand) diagram indicates how the pattern will appear if the music is staccato or marcato. The following instructions and diagrams are useble in any ensemble setting, whether vocal or instrumental.

In all conducting patterns the first beat of the pattern is a downward motion and the last beat of the pattern is upward. In the basic three-beat pattern, beat 2 is to the right of the conductor. Therefore the pattern is down (beat 1), right (beat 2), and up (beat 3). This pattern is used for music in time signatures of 3/4, 3/8, 9/8, and 3/2 and is appropriate for any triple meter work.

Example 4.2
Three pattern—legato style and staccato style.

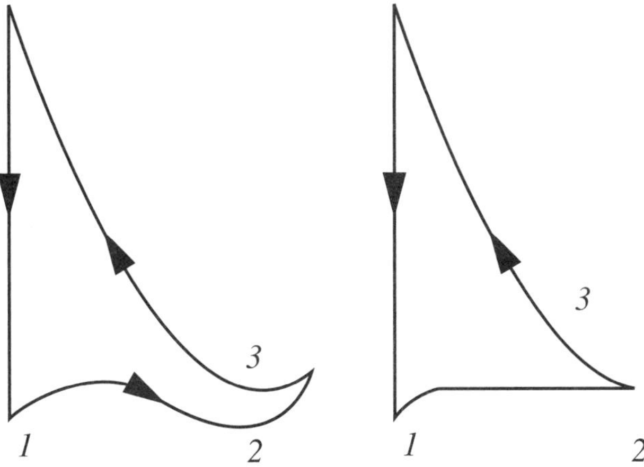

Exercise 4.1 ***Come, Sweet Death,*** J. S. Bach

Exercise 4.2 ***Sing We and Chant It,*** Thomas Morley

Exercise 4.3 ***Les Preludes,*** Franz Liszt

Example 4.3
Two pattern—
legato and staccato.

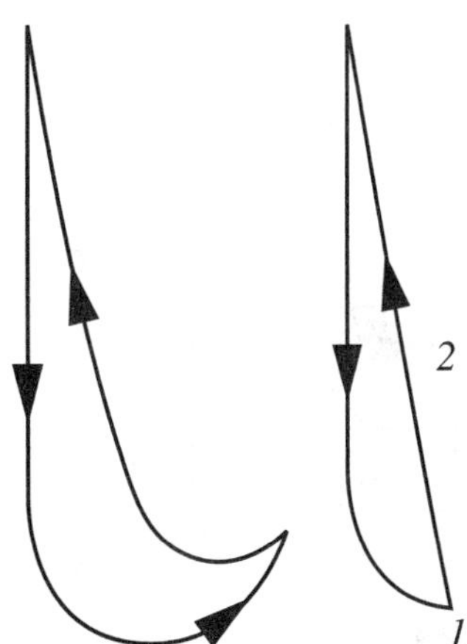

The two-beat pattern is the simplest, being only a downward motion (beat 1) followed by an upward motion (beat 2). As shown in Example 4-3, the pattern is usually executed in a backward "J" shape with a slight outward movement to the conductor's right. This pattern is used for 2/4, 2/2, "cut time," and any pattern of two. The conductor should be careful not to allow the rebound of beat 1 to be so high that the pattern begins to look like a "U" rather than a backward "J."

Exercise 4.4 ***Petite Symphonie, mvt .4,*** Charles Gounod

Exercise 4.5 ***Symphony No. 8 mvt. 4,*** Antony Dvořák

Exercise 4.6 ***Carmen,*** George Bizet

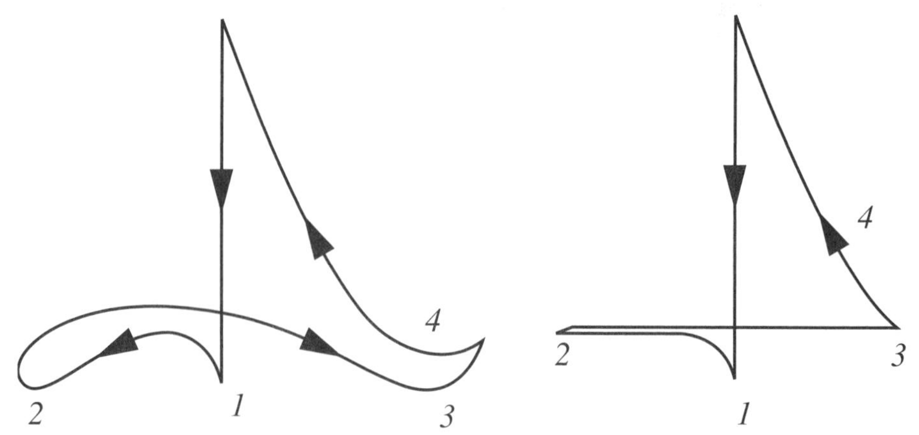

Example 4.4
Four pattern—legato and staccato.

The most commonly used pattern is the four pattern. This pattern is most often used for works with 4/4, 12/8, and 4/2 time signatures but can be used for any meter that has a repetitive pattern of four pulses.

In the four pattern the conductor should move to the left for the second beat of the pattern and to the right for the third beat. This creates a pattern movement of down (beat 1), left (beat 2), right (beat 3), and up (beat 4).

Exercise 4.7 ***Ave Verum Corpus,*** Wolfgang Amadeus Mozart

Exercise 4.8 ***Symphony No.9, mvt. IV,*** Ludwig van Beethoven

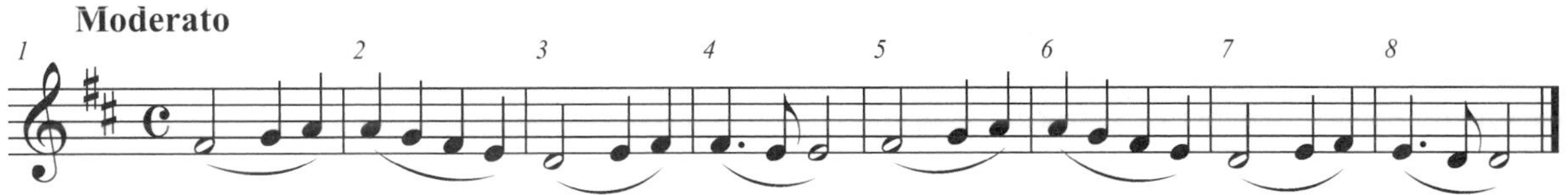

Exercise 4.9 ***The Messiah, Hallelujah Chorus,*** George Frideric Handel

Exercise 4.9 *(continued)*

Exercise 4.10 *Slavonic Dance No.5,* Antonin Dvořák

Exercises 4.11, 4.12, and 4.13 provide further practice for two- and three-beat patterns.

Exercise 4.11 *Symphony No. 104, mvt. 1,* Franz Joseph Haydn

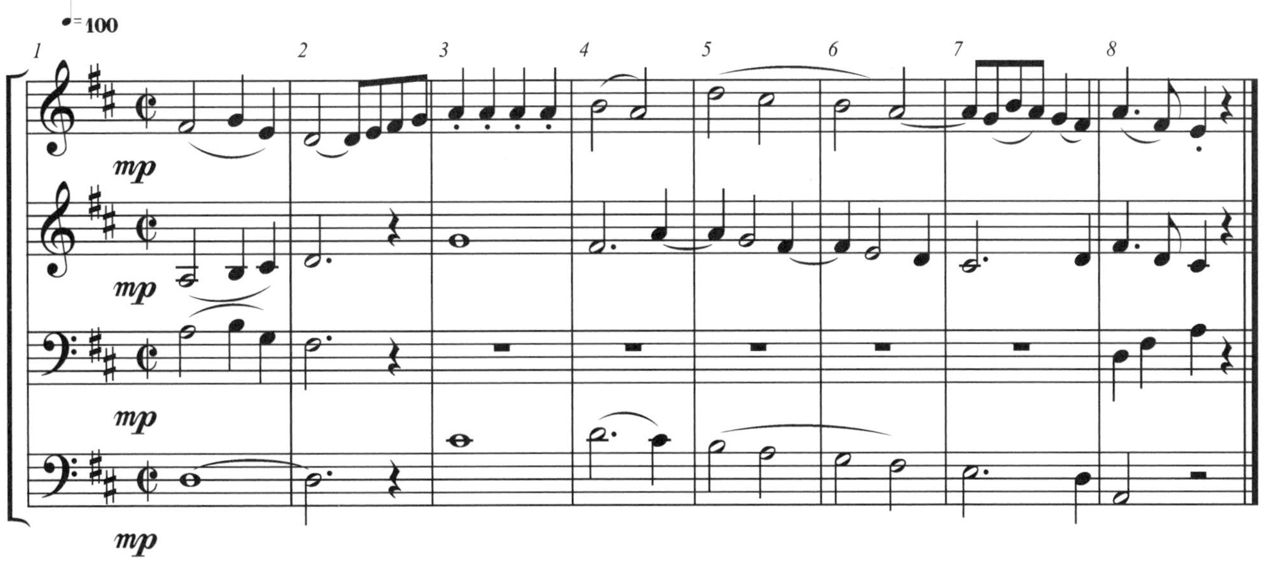

Exercise 4.12 *L'Orfeo, "Chorus,"* Claudio Monteverdi

Exercise 4.13 *The Merry Widow Waltz,* Franz Lehar

Some music is so fast that, regardless of the meter, it is best conducted in one beat per bar. The shape of this pattern is governed by the length of time of rebound appropriate to the style of the music. Exercise 4.14 requires little time for the rebound motion. In this instance the conductor should give repeated downbeats, with the rebound action being one half of the amount of time of a measure. Exercise 4.15 will also be given with repeated downbeats. However, the length of time of the rebound, and perhaps the size of the rebound, will be longer in this exercise than in Exercise 4.14 because the work must retain a three feel within the one beat per bar. The crispness of the rebound will also be more in Exercise 4.15 than in Exercise 4.14 because of the articulation.

Exercise 4.14 *Symphony No. 5, mvt. 1,* Ludwig van Beethoven

Exercise 4.15 *Carmen, Act IV,* Georges Bizet

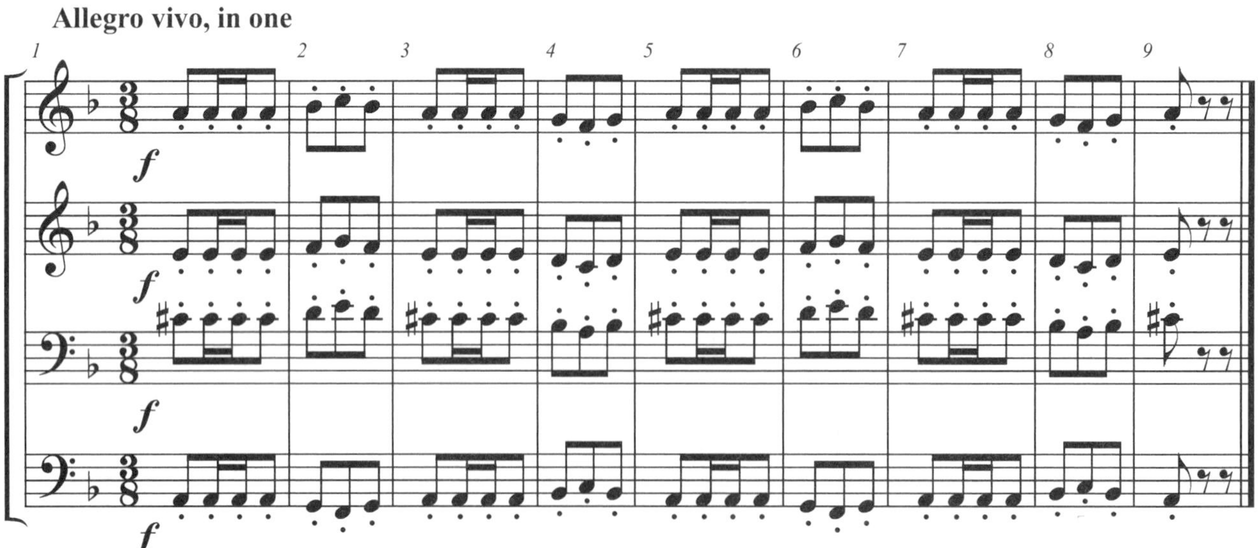

Beginning conductors often think of less common or asymmetrical patterns, such as five or seven, as difficult or complex. In reality they are simply combination patterns of the simpler patterns of two, three, or four. For example, a work in 5/4 or 5/8 time can usually be conducted by combining the more common patterns of two and three. Often in the cases of 5/8 or 7/8, one of the beats of a common pattern is elongated. For example, if a 5/8 pattern is notated as a grouping of two eighth notes followed by a grouping of three eighth notes, the conductor could conduct a 2 pattern and elongate beat two. The music itself dictates the combination pattern. The conductor must analyze the rhythmic structure of the music and choose a beat pattern that matches this structure.

Example 4.5
Five pattern—2 + 3 and 3 + 2.

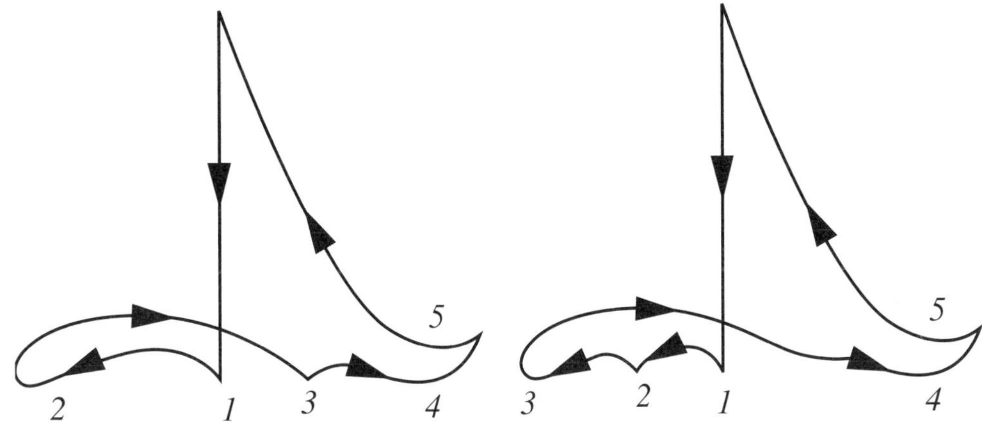

Exercise 4.16 ***Symphony No. 6, mvt. II,*** Pyotr Ilyich Tchaikovsky

Exercise 4.16 *Continued*

Exercise 4.17

♩= 160

1 2 3 4

p p p p

♩= 160

5 6 7 8

p p p p

Exercise 4.18 ***Pictures at an Exhibition,*** Modest Mussorgsky

Allegro giusto

Exercise 4.19 ***Symphony No. 3, mvt. 2,*** Alexander Borodin

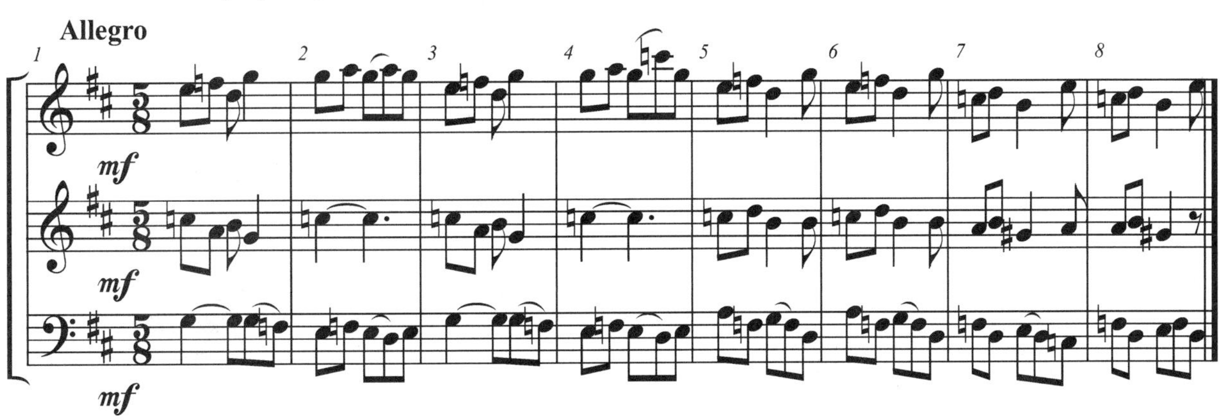

The same is true of the patterns in seven.

Example 4.6
Seven pattern—
3 + 4 and 4 + 3.

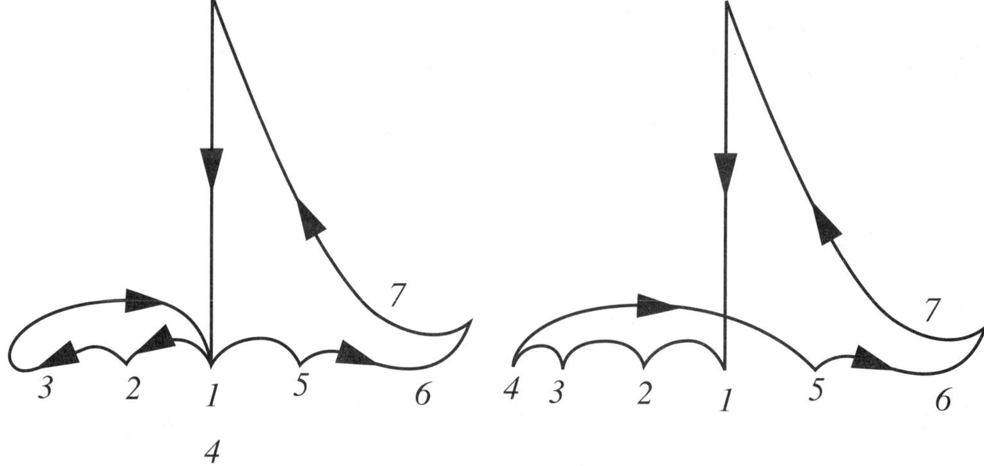

Exercise 4.20

Exercise 4.21 *War Requiem, Dies irae,* Benjamin Britten

Exercise 4.22

♩= 100

1 2 3 4

mf *mf* *mf* *mf*

5 6 7 8

Exercise 4.23 *Orchestral Variations, V. 15,* Aaron Copland

The six-beat patterns are most commonly used for passages at a slow tempo in 6/8 meter but of course can be used for any music in which the meter is based on six. The most commonly used six-beat pattern is a combination of three beats first on the left side of the conductor's body and then three beats on the right.

The only other commonly used six-beat pattern alternates the icti from the left to the right of the vertical plane.

Example 4.7
Six pattern.

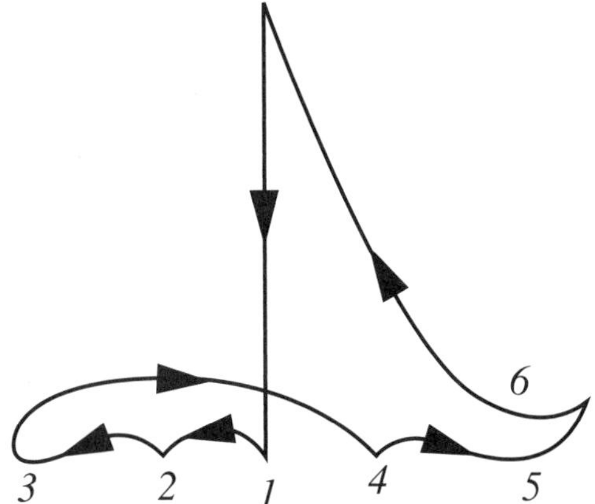

Exercise 4.24 ***Symphony No. 6, mvt.5,*** Ludwig van Beethoven

Exercise 4.25 should be conducted in two beats per bar because of the tempo.

Exercise 4.25 ***Symphony No. 4, mvt.1,*** Felix Mendelssohn

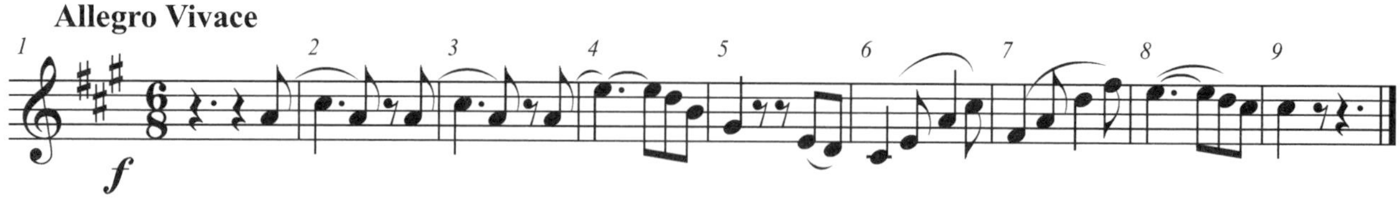

Exercise 4.26 ***Symphony No. 5, mvt.2,*** Franz Schubert

Exercise 4.27 *Symphony No. 4, mvt. 2,* Johannes Brahms

Exercise 4.28 *Symphony No. 3, mvt. 1,* Johannes Brahms

Exercise 4.29 ***The Sunken Cathedral,*** Claude Debussy

A good deal of music does not begin on the first beat of a measure. The following exercises prepare the conductor to conduct what are commonly called "pick-up" beats. Like all preparatory beats, the prep beat for such excerpts should simply be the beat immediately preceding the first sounded beat of music. For example, in Exercise 4.30 the conductor should give count 1 to the ensemble as the preparatory beat (assuming he intends to conduct this exercise in two). Exercise 4.31 requires that the conductor give the downbeat of the first measure as the prep beat.

Exercise 4.30 ***"Trout" Quintet in A major,*** Franz Schubert

Exercise 4.31 *Irish Tune*

Exercise 4.32 *Symphony No. 6, mvt. 3,* Ludwig van Beethoven

Exercise 4.33 *Brandenberg Concerto No. 2, mvt. 2,* J. S. Bach

Exercise 4.33 *Continued*

In Exercises 4.34, 4.35, and 4.36 the conductor will need to give two preparatory beats to the ensemble because the music begins on an "up beat." When so doing the conductor must give one preparatory beat that is a "dead beat" or passive gesture and one that is a "live beat" or active gesture. The first of these two gestures helps establish the tempo. The second confirms the tempo and provides all the other information that normal prep beats offer. If a conductor gives two "live" beats, the performers will be confused and will attempt to enter after the first of the two prep beats.

Exercise 4.34 *Symphony No. 94, mvt. 4,* Franz Joseph Haydn

Exercise 4.35 *Symphony No. 4, mvt. 1,* Felix Mendelssohn

Exercise 4.36 ***Sleepers Awake!,*** J. S. Bach

The beginning conductor should be conscious of the amount of rebound used in the pattern and the horizontal distance between icti. Excessive rebound and insufficient horizontal distance between icti cause patterns to be unclear. Some conducting texts actually recommend that all icti of a pattern happen at the same spot, but this causes a looping kind of pattern and is not recommended.

BASIC RELEASES

The type of release used is dictated by the style of the music. The shape or type of gesture is usually determined by the length of decay of sound required in the music.

Releases can be made with the baton hand, the left hand, or both, depending on the situation. The one basic rule of a release gesture is that it must leave the hands/arms in position for the next musical sound. This is especially important to remember when releasing fermata.

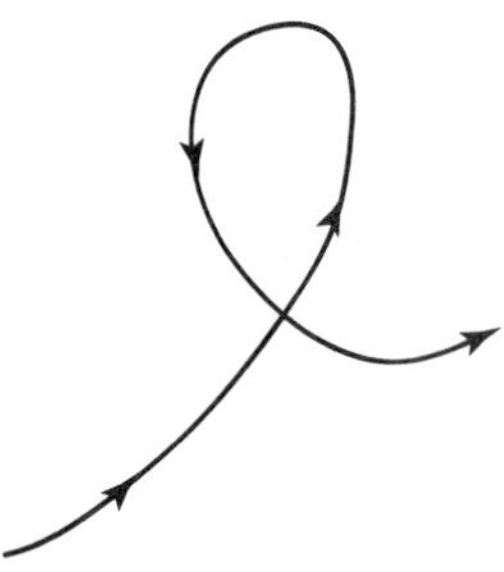

Example 4.8
Right-hand release.

The simplest release is the circular baton release. This release can be used in most situations and can be performed in a variety of styles. It is most useful to cut off an extended pitch or a fermata. The release is performed by a combination of an upward circular motion followed by an ictus made with a downward motion. The gesture should accelerate toward the ictus. The baton hand can move in either a clockwise or counterclockwise direction in the release, and this can be determined best by practicing both directions to find which seems most natural. This release can also be mirrored with the left hand. When using a mirror circular release, the hands must rotate in opposite directions. The size of this gesture should be dictated by the dynamic level of the music; the louder the music, the larger the gesture.

Much instrumental music ends with what is often referred to as a "stinger note" or "bop note," which is a short and accented final pitch. This type of ending also requires a release even though the ensemble will stop playing without the conductor giving one. An appropriate release gesture is to beat the ictus of the final beat with a full stop. The length of rebound, if any, will indicate to the performers if the sound should be stopped abruptly or have an element of decay.

Not all releases happen at the ends of works. Releases after fermata or at breath marks and caesura also require attention.

A release before a breath mark, usually indicated by a comma in the music, requires that the conductor stop on the ictus prior to the comma and, after a short hesitation, continue on in the direction of the next beat.

The caesura creates more break in the music than does the breath mark. To release a caesura the conductor should perform a circular baton release back toward the ictus prior to the caesura. Then, he should rebeat that same ictus as a prep beat in order to continue.

USE OF THE LEFT HAND FOR RELEASES

Using the left hand to perform releases gives the conductor many more options, and these are especially useful for releases that require a delicate touch. These left-handed gestures are often more in character with the music since the fingers can be used.

> A very useful left hand release is a clockwise gesture with the elbow and wrist while closing the fingers of the left hand to the thumb (not into a fist).
>
> An even smoother gesture can be created by a gesture of rolling the fingers closed while appearing to grasp an imaginary object in mid air. This gives the impression of gathering the sound out of the air to cause the release.
>
> A more forceful left-handed gesture can be created by extending the left hand as if to shake hands, moving upward and at the same time in a circular motion while closing the fingers onto the thumb.

All releases need some kind of preparation or the ensemble will be taken by surprise. Much like a prep beat, the conductor must indicate with the gesture where to end the note. This is usually accomplished by ending the gesture on the ictus of the final beat with a prep gesture immediately leading into that final gesture.

Exercises 4.37 through 4.41 provide opportunity for practicing different styles of releases.

Exercise 4.37

Exercise 4.38 ***Blessed Are They,*** Johannes Brahms

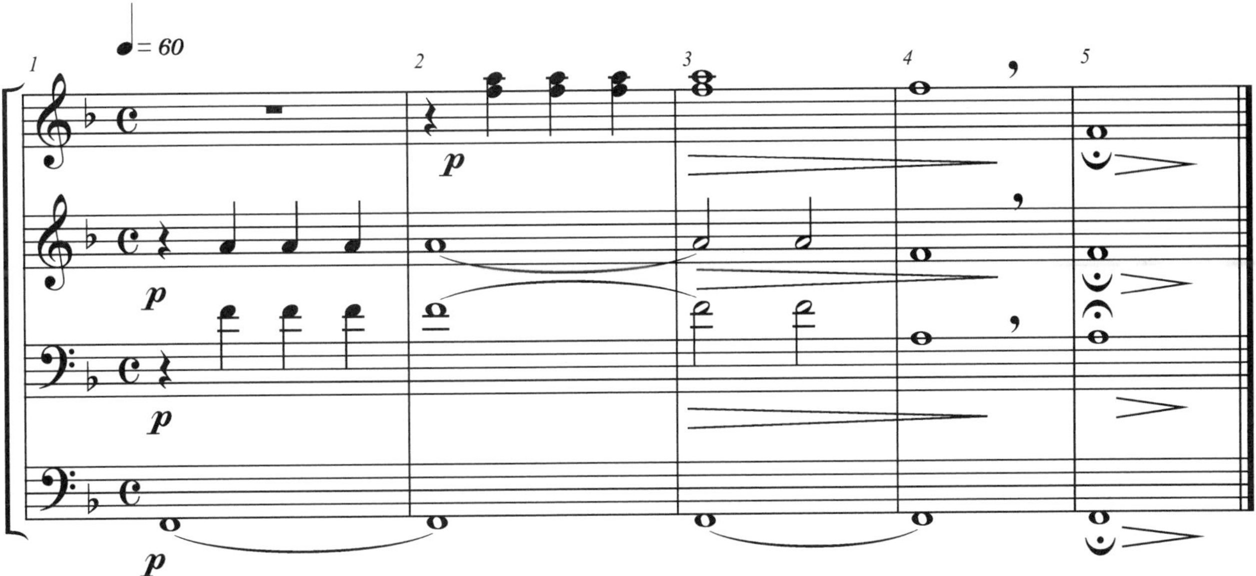

Exercise 4.39 ***Nessun Dorma,*** Giacomo Puccini

Exercise 4.40 *Symphony No. 5,* Ludwig van Beethoven

Exercise 4.41 *The Washington Post March,* J. P. Sousa

SUBDIVISION OF BEATS

In some music the conductor will need to indicate the subdivisions of the beat as well as the primary pulses. This usually occurs when the tempo is so slow that it is uncomfortable or looks unnatural to conduct the pulse. The conductor may also find subdivision useful in the conducting of ritards.

The most successful manner of conducting these half beats is the "rebound style." In this pattern the conductor rebounds off the primary ictus of the beat and rebounds back to rebeat that same ictus before traveling to the next beat. The rebound style is shown in Example 4.9.

Example 4.9
Rebound—style subdivision.

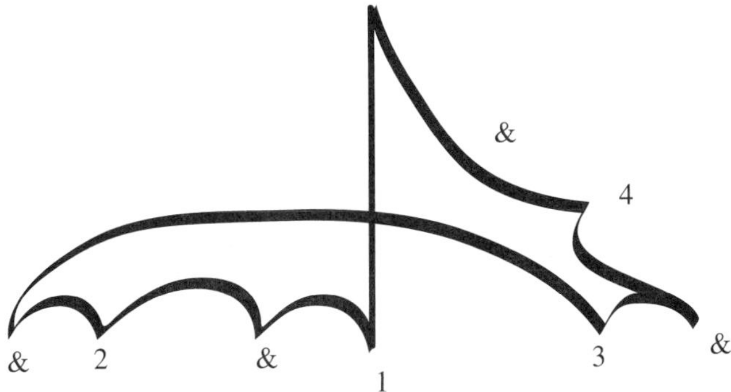

The rebound ictus, or subdivided beat, should be smaller in gesture than the primary beat.

Another style of subdivided pattern is created by conducting full stops (or no rebound) on each beat and each subdivision of the subdivided pattern. The subdivided beats will occur during what would ordinarily be the rebound of the primary beat. This style of pattern is best used in marcato or staccato style music. Example 4-10 illustrates this type of subdivided pattern.

Example 4.10
Subdivided beat,
no rebound.

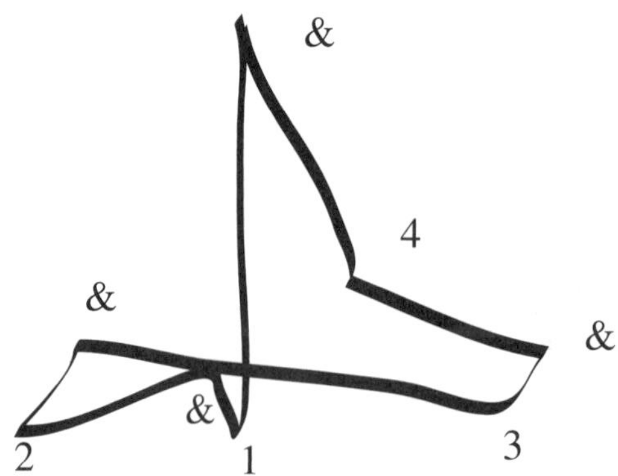

Exercises 4.42 and 4.43 should be conducted with subdivided patterns.

Exercise 4.42 ***Pavan,*** William Byrd

Exercise 4.43 ***Serenade in B-flat, mvt. 3,*** Wolfgang Amadeus Mozart

UNIT 2

Advanced Techniques

CHAPTER 5

Advanced Techniques

While titled "advanced techniques," each of the movements suggested in this chapter is an essential tool of communication for the conductor. They assume mastery of beat pattern and stance.

ARTICULATION AND STYLE

In order to indicate to the ensemble the style of sound required, the conductor must be able to control and alter the basic pattern shape and how fast or slowly the baton moves from one ictus point to another. (The distance between ictus points is called "travel.") Two primary and rather general styles exist: the legato style and the angular style.

The legato style of conducting is used when the music is of a lyrical nature. The wrist is the most important hinge used to create a legato style. To perform any pattern in this style, the conductor simply combines rounded pattern direction changes at the ictus points with smooth and steady travel between ictus points. This creates a pattern that appears smooth and that indicates to performers that they should play in a lyrical, flowing style. Legato style is much easier to accomplish at a moderate tempo. It is difficult for most young conductors to accomplish a true legato style at extremely slow tempi. When practicing legato style, try it first at moderate speeds and then gradually slow the tempo. The student might also be aided by imagining that the arms are moving through water from ictus to ictus. The movement of the wrist hinge is very important in the proper production of a legato style. Generally speaking, the wrist should lead the arm and baton through the pattern. Conducting the pattern with a "broken" wrist and allowing the baton tip to follow behind the wrist, even through direction changes, creates a very good legato style. A simple exercise to aid in the development of legato style is to imagine the painting of a wall in a slow up and down fashion without removing the brush from the wall. This action will mimic the downbeat and upbeat motion in a legato pattern. The same exercise moving the imaginary paint brush from left to right creates the motion of counts two and three of a four-beat pattern. The following exercises make use of the legato technique of conducting.

Exercise 5.1 ***Salvation Is Created,*** Pavel Tschesnokoff

Exercise 5.2 ***Blessed Are They,*** Johannes Brahms

♩= 60

1 2 3 4 5 6

p

p

p

p

7 8 9 10 11 12

The angular style is used primarily for passages that are marked staccato or marcato. A staccato style of conducting requires that the pattern direction changes be angular in nature and more marked than in legato style. The travel in a staccato style is fast, and usually the baton makes a full stop on each ictus point. This stop is created with the wrist hinge, sometimes with a "flick" of the wrist. The conductor can practice this flick by imagining that he is flicking a water droplet off the tip of the baton.

Exercise 5.3 ***Slavonic Dances,*** Antonin Dvořák

Exercise 5.4 ***George Washington Bridge,*** William Schuman

Exercise 5.4 *Continued*

Marcato style is similar to staccato in that the pattern is a series of full stop ictus points. To create a marcato pattern, the conductor uses less wrist movement (usually no flick) and more arm/shoulder movement. Each ictus must have an accented full stop gesture with very little rebound. To simulate the motion required in marcato style, the conductor might practice using the baton in a jabbing motion. This exercise usually makes one employ the elbow hinge to create the jab, which is important in producing a true marcato.

Exercise 5.5 *Symphonie Fantastique,* Hector Berlioz

Exercise 5.6 *Triumphal March from "Aida,"* Giuseppe Verdi

Pesante style is a combination of the marcato and legato styles. It contains the smooth, slow travel of legato with the heavy arm movement and accented ictus points of marcato. There is little wrist movement, and the conductor creates the pattern from the shoulder hinge or a combination of shoulder and elbow hinges. The conductor might practice imagining the movement of a very heavy box or weight from one ictus point to the next, setting the weight down heavily at each ictus point.

Exercise 5.7 *The Great Gate of Kiev,* Modest Mussorgsky

Exercise 5.8 *Carmina Burana, O Fortuna,* Carl Orff

DYNAMICS

It is also important that the conductor indicate the proper dynamics to the ensemble. This is done in part with the size of the pattern. (Other methods of indicating dynamics are discussed later in this chapter and in Chapter 6.) The size of the pattern can be altered either by using more or less of the gesture box or by using various hinges to create a different size pattern. Most often, the two go together.

The softer the sound, the smaller the gesture/pattern. The conductor should continually alter the size of the pattern as the dynamics change. Gestures to indicate soft sounds are usually produced with the hand and wrist. For louder sounds conductors usually use the elbow and shoulder hinges. As the conductor uses more shoulder and elbow motion, the amount of wrist and finger movement must decrease. Otherwise the performer sees too many hinge points in motion at once and the pattern often takes on a whipping kind of movement.

Dynamics change either abruptly or gradually. Often an isolated note has a sudden dynamic change or accent that must be indicated. When called upon to point out an isolated accented pitch, the conductor must give the appropriate gesture both as a prep beat to an accented note and on the note itself. For example, in order to indicate the accented pitch on count 1, the conductor must prepare the sound on beat 4 of the preceding measure by giving a marcato style gesture and follow that up with the same gesture on beat 1.

Subito dynamic changes or terraced dynamic changes require the same type of preparatory beat. The conductor must always remember to give the change in style prior to the actual performance of the change.

Crescendi and diminuendi can be indicated with the baton hand alone by simply changing the size of the pattern. Use of the left hand in conjunction with this size change is recommended and discussed later in this chapter.

Exercise 5.9 ***Canon in D,*** Johann Pachelbel

Exercise 5.9 ***Continued***

Exercise 5.10 ***Canzon duo decimi toni,*** Giovanni Gabrieli

Exercise 5.11 ***Symphony No. 3, Finale,*** Gustav Mahler

Exercise 5.12 ***Hymnsong,*** **Philip Bliss**

Exercise 5.13 *First Suite in E-flat, Intermezzo,* Gustav Holst

♩ = 120

mf

mf

mf

mf

Exercise 5.14 *Prelude in c minor,* Frederick Chopin

ACCENTED PITCHES

The conductor often wants to emphasize an accented note with a gesture. These might be notes that are dynamically accented or punctuated by a percussion instrument or special instrumental technique. The gesture for such an isolated accented pitch must visually stand out from the other beats/gestures around it. Just like an entrance, this accent must have a preparatory gesture that communicates the articulation and dynamic emphasis relative to the notes surrounding it. In order to emphasize the prep gesture and the accented gesture itself, the conductor might decrease the size of the preceding pattern and then increase the size of the pattern during the prep and accented note. It will be most effective if the left hand is used in conjunction with the right during the prep gesture and the accented gesture.

CUES

Cues are preparatory gestures given by the conductor that assist the entrance of a performer. They are usually given following a long series of rests, upon the first entrance of the performer(s) in a work, when a solo part enters, or whenever reassurance from the conductor will aid the performance. Cues can be given with the baton hand, the left hand, the head, or the eyes. Often a combination of these works best.

Cues, like all other gestures, must be prepared. It does very little good to suddenly throw out your left hand in the general direction of a player at the start of the player's line. In order to deliver a good cue, the conductor should first look at the performer(s) in question and gain eye contact. Without this, the cue will be of no value. This eye contact should happen far enough in advance of the required entrance for the performer and conductor to feel confidant that the entrance will be made. Usually this is several beats ahead of the entrance. The cue must be given a preparatory beat in the style and dynamic of the entrance. Often the cue is given outside (usually higher) the normal pattern plane. This helps draw attention to the cue. The facial expression (discussed in depth in Chapter 6) is an important part of the cue. It must also indicate the general style of the music to be performed and should be of a reassuring nature.

Cues given by the baton hand must not interrupt the regular pulse of the pattern. Right-hand cues are best given higher than the usual plane of the pattern, and the beats of the pattern immediately preceding the cue should be smaller in size in order to focus more attention on the cue when it is given.

Left-hand cues have the advantage that the pattern is not disrupted. Several beats prior to the cue, the left hand should be brought from the rest position to a high level in the plane. The left hand can deliver a more gentle style of cue than the right because it does not have the baton. A good left hand cue is to bring the arm up to high plane position, palm facing the ensemble, and round the fingers of the hand so that the thumb and forefinger touch with all fingers slightly curved. Give the prep beat for the cue with the elbow or wrist hinge, and on the beat where the performer should enter pull the thumb and forefinger apart with the other fingers following the forefinger. (This cue is more easily produced than described and will be a natural and fluid motion when tried.)

A head cue is simply a reassuring nod. The same type and level of gesture can be given with the eyes and eyebrows. These types of cues are to be used when both the conductor and performer are confidant of the performance and all that is needed is the "ok, go ahead" sign. Large or repeated movements of the head are not effective and will appear out of place with the music. Head and eye movements are often combined with either left- or right-hand cues.

The beginning conductor is cautioned to not overcue the ensemble or he will begin to look like a traffic cop and other musically important issues suffer.

Exercise 5.15 ***Serenade, Op. 44,*** Antonin Dvořák

Exercise 5.16 ***Serenade in B-flat, "Gran Partita,"*** Wolfgang Amadeus Mozart

Exercise 5.17

Exercise 5.18

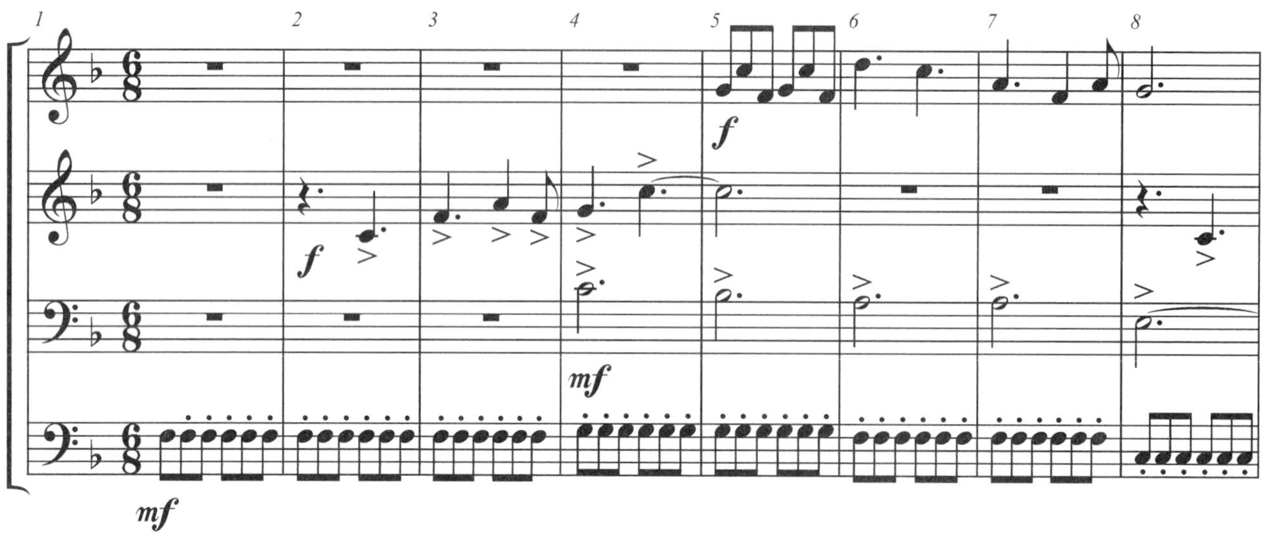

FERMATA

Fermata are used by composers to create a particular dramatic effect, usually to draw attention to the next musical event. Because of this the primary fermata problems for conductors are what to do physically during the fermata and how to get out of them gracefully.

In order to cause the performer to continue the sound during a fermata, the conductor must give some type of active gesture. This could be a very slow movement of the baton hand (travel), a slight movement of the body toward the ensemble, or a position of hands and arms that implies movement. Whatever is used, the conductor cannot simply remain motionless with a passive expression or the performers will stop playing. If the conductor uses travel to sustain the fermata, it should continue in the general direction of the beat on which the fermata is placed.

The gesture used to release a fermata depends on what music follows it, and the end of the release gesture must put the conductor's arm/hands in the proper position to continue. Fermata are followed by silence or sound (obviously). But the length of the silence or the type of the sound makes a significant difference in how the fermata is ended. If the fermata is like that in Example 5.19, where all performers stop together and continue on together, the conductor can simply decide whether or not there should be a break between the fermata and the next note. If there should not be a break, the conductor gives a preparatory beat in the tempo and style of the next beat without any type of cut-off gesture. This prep beat should look like a small and smooth rebeating of the beat of the fermata. For example, if the fermata is on beat 3 and the conductor wants no break, he should rebeat count 3 as a prep beat and give no release gesture.

If there should be a break in sound between the fermata note and the next note, the conductor should make the cut-off and the preparatory beat in the same gesture. Near the end of the fermata, the conductor prepares the release by speeding up the travel, executing one of the release gestures suggested in Chapter 4 while simultaneously giving the prep beat for the following note. These fermata are best handled with two hands, giving the release gesture in the left hand and the prep gesture for the next note with the right hand. The release gesture should include a movement that appears to be a rebeating of the fermata beat in order that the prep beat occurs on the correct beat of the pattern. For example, in the Exercise 5.24 the conductor releases the fermata with a re-beating of count 3 as a prep beat for continuing on to beat 4.

In some cases not all performers stop at the same time, meaning that there will be two or more fermata in the same measure. If the conductor wants to indicate anything but the final fermata of the measure (and it is not necessary to do so), it is best to do this with the use of both hands. Generally, it is best to use the left hand to indicate the first fermata and the baton hand to carry the beat pattern forward, allowing it to be used for the final fermata of the measure. In Example 5.20 the conductor should indicate the first fermata with the left hand while continuing on to beat with in the pattern with the right hand.

Silences after fermata are of four types: fermata that ends the work, fermata followed by a breath mark (short break), fermata followed by a caesura (longer break), or fermata followed by a grand pause. In all of these cases except the fermata followed by a breath mark, the conductor can simply use an appropriate release, pause the appropriate amount of time, and continue on by giving a prep beat appropriate to the next musical sound. However, the breath mark or short pause may best be executed, as suggested above, by combining the fermata release gesture with preparatory gesture causing a short break or lift between the two notes. This same type of gesture can be used where there is a caesura but no fermata.

Exercise 5.19 *Trial by Jury,* Arthur Sullivan

♩= 132

1 2 3 4

mf

mf

mf

mf

5 6 7 8

Exercise 5.20 *In Thy Bosom Receive Me*

Exercise 5.21 *Symphony No. 5, mvt. 1,* Ludwig van Beethoven

Exercise 5.22 *The Star Spangled Banner*

Exercise 5.22 *Continued*

Exercise 5.23 *Overture for Band,* Felix Mendelssohn

Exercise 5.24 *Christ, He Is My Life,* J. S. Bach

TENUTO

A tenuto marking usually indicates the lengthening of a particular note, but not to the extent that a fermata is needed. A tenuto breaks the steady pulse of the rhythm but does not bring it to a full stop. The same must happen with the conducting gesture. To execute a tenuto the conductor simply extends the rebound or travel of the beat on which the tenuto is placed, making one beat of the pattern larger. This gesture is aided by slowing down the travel and causing it to look as if there is resistance to the travel (perhaps visualize your hands moving thick mud). The gesture should not require a prep beat in order to continue unless some type of caesura is indicated after the tenuto.

Exercise 5.25 ***America the Beautiful,*** Samuel Ward

TEMPO FLUCTUATION AND MAINTENANCE

Setting and maintaining the proper tempo is one of the most important tasks for the conductor. In fact, some writers about conducting, such as Richard Wagner, claim it to be the only job of the conductor.

ESTABLISHING AND MAINTAINING A TEMPO

Tempo is the relationship between two beats/pulses. In order to establish a tempo, the conductor must give at least two pulses. The tempo will be set by performers perceiving the relationship in time between the preparatory ictus and the ictus of the first beat of the music. For example, a slow preparatory gesture with slow travel will indicate a slow tempo.

For many conductors the setting of tempo is difficult. Often they have a good idea of the accurate tempo in their head but do not relay that to the ensemble through their gestures. This is usually caused by lack of control of the arms and can be addressed through practicing preparatory beats and patterns with the aid of a metronome. The conductor should first hear the tempo in his head for several beats before trying to create the actual conducting gestures. This focusing on pulse internally will help the conductor gain control of the physical movements.

Maintaining a steady tempo is far more difficult than setting one. The ability to maintain tempo and listen to your own internal metronome while those around you continually attempt variation is a skill that must be developed over time. The conductor's time clock is assailed by slight tempo variations of individual performers, wrong entrances, audience interruptions, and other external negative factors. Score preparation is usually the best route to tempo maintenance. If a conductor has a very accurate internal idea of the sound of the work, tempo variations are easier to detect and counteract. Working with a metronome will help develop this skill.

Exercise 5.26 ***Overture to the Marriage of Figaro,*** Wolfgang Amadeus Mozart

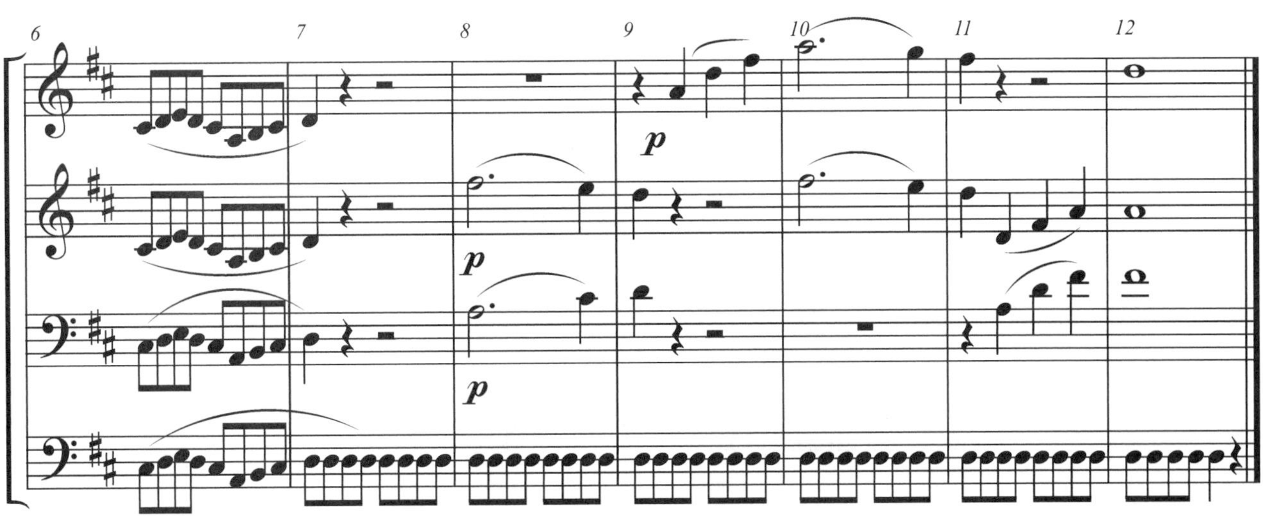

Exercise 5.27 ***Symphony No. 94, mvt. 4,*** Franz Joseph Haydn

Exercise 5.28 ***If Thou Be Near,*** J. S. Bach

TEMPO FLUCTUATIONS

Intended alterations of tempo such as accelerando, ritardando, or subito tempo changes must be prepared by the conductor. Generally speaking, all changes of tempo require some prepared indication from the conductor, and all require that the conductor actually be beating a pattern or pulse at a different tempo than the one being played. This is so that the conductor's gesture is always ahead of the ensemble and shows the ensemble what their next sound should be. Ritards and accelerandi can be accomplished by changing the travel speed and are often accompanied by a change in size of pattern to gain attention to the change. Often when slowing the tempo, the conductor makes the pattern more legato in style, and when accelerating the pattern can become more staccato in nature. It is important to make eye contact with the ensemble prior to the tempo change. By making some change in the pattern—either the size or by mirroring with the left hand—the conductor alerts the ensemble to the fact that something is about to change. Then, at the proper moment the conductor begins the change BEFORE it actually must happen as a preparatory for the ensemble.

Exercise 5.29 ***Canzon duo decimi toni,*** Giovanni Gabrieli

Exercise 5.30 ***1812 Overture,*** Pyotr Ilyich Tchaikovsky

sempre rallentanto al Largo

Largo

Exercise 5.31 ***Pineapple Poll, mvt. 4,*** Arthur Sullivan

Exercise 5.32 ***The Merry Widow,*** Franz Lehar

PREP BEATS FOR SYNCOPATED ENTRANCES

Any gesture that elicits a syncopated entrance or accent must occur on the pulse prior to the syncopation. Elizabeth Green, in her book *The Modern Conductor*,[1] called this the "Gesture of Syncopation." This gesture is defined as a full stop of the pattern on the ictus prior to the syncopated note. Such a gesture is very effective in creating a syncopated entrance. The harder the gesture, or full stop, the more accented the note will be. The conductor should not rebound off the ictus point, and often an increase in the speed of travel toward the ictus will make the gesture of syncopation clearer. This gesture is also sometimes used to indicate the end of notes that are tied over a barline.

If a work begins with a syncopated rhythm, or the ensemble enters after a long pause on a syncopated line, the conductor will need to give two preparatory beats. The first beat given is a normal prep beat showing tempo, style, and dynamics. The second prep beat becomes the full stop, syncopated gesture and will cause the ensemble to perform the syncopation.

Exercise 5.33 ***Song of the Blacksmith***

Exercise 5.33 *Continued*

Exercise 5.34 *Symphony No. 5, mvt. 1,* Ludwig van Beethoven

Exercise 5.35

♩= 100

1 2 3 4

mf

mf

mf

mf

5 6 7 8

Exercise 5.36 *Petite Symphonie, mvt. 2,* Charles Gounod

Exercise 5.36 *Continued*

Exercise 5.37 *Sleepers Awake,* J. S. Bach

MIXED PATTERNS

A good deal of music contains changes of meter. The conductor must be able to easily and naturally change the pattern in order to lead the ensemble. Three types of pattern changes exist: changes where the basic pulse stays the same and only the number of beats in a measure is altered, changes where the pulse and meter change but there is some relationship between the old and new pulse, and changes where the pulse and meter change and there is no apparent relationship in pulse.

Simply a change in meter should not present large challenges to the conductor who has mastered the different conducting patterns. Refer to Exercise 5-33 and the following exercises for examples of this type of mixed pattern.

Exercise 5.38 ***Remembrance,*** Warren Benson

Exercise 5.39 *Shenandoah*

Exercise 5.40 *Trial by Jury,* Arthur Sullivan

♩= 132

mf

f

A change of meter that also has a relational pulse can be more difficult for the conductor to perform. Understanding of the rhythmic structure and relationship as well as a good internal clock is essential to smooth execution of these changes.

Exercise 5.41 ***Postcard,*** Frank Tlcheli
(Courtesy of www.ManhattanBeachMusic.com)

Perhaps the hardest meter change to accomplish is one where there is no apparent relationship in tempo between the old meter and the new. This occurs frequently in opera and musical scores. The conductor must be able to show the new pulse and speed one beat prior to the ensemble executing the change while the ensemble is still playing in the old tempo and meter.

Exercise 5.42 ***Excerpts from "Oklahoma,"*** Richard Rodgers

Exercise 5.42 ***Continued***

UNMETERED AND TIMED MEASURES

Much contemporary music contains passages that do not require standard patterns of conducting. These passages usually contain no meter, or the meter does not adequately express the musical intent, or the passages are to be accomplished in a given number of seconds. Often the notation is of an iconic nature and the rhythmic notation is proportional notation. Sometimes the duration of these passages is left to the performer or the conductor. In each of these situations the conductor makes use of standard gestures and patterns but modifies them to fit the situation. Many of the actual gestures used may be "cue-like" in nature.

In unmetered works the conductor might use the downbeat gesture as the primary method of directing each event or note. It is generally not a good idea to impose a beat pattern upon a work that the composer has left unmetered. Doing so tends to cause the players to perform certain weak and strong notes, which actually then create a meter where none is indicated.

In a score that requires certain measures or sections to be of particular length in seconds or minutes, the use of a watch is essential, perhaps even at the performance. Many entrances or events are numbered, and the conductor might use left hand fingers to indicate each cued entrance.

Exercise 5.43 *Lord Melbourne*

Exercise 5.44 *Crystals,* Thomas C. Duffy

USE OF THE LEFT HAND

The conductor must learn to use the left hand such that its gestures do not interfere with or alter the right hand's movements in any way. The left hand is most used for expressive purposes. Conductors often rely on the left hand to show shadings of dynamics, articulation, and style. The left hand is also often used for cueing. However, just like the right hand, it can be used for both beat pattern and expression.

The normal at-rest position for the left hand is hanging in a relaxed fashion at the side. The conductor should only bring the left hand up to within the conducting plane when he wants the ensemble to respond to it or at the beginning of each piece of music (see Ready Position in Chapter 3.) Having the left hand visible to the players at all times trains them to not pay attention to it. The conductor should use the left hand in an intentional manner to achieve a certain effect.

In most cases the left hand, when in the conducting plane, should be shaped with fingers together, and in most cases the fingers should be curved in a relaxed and natural fashion. Spreading of the fingers or tightly closing the fingers looks odd to players and does not convey focus or intent. Because the left hand does not contain a baton, it has the ability to imitate the sensation of touch better than the right. The conductor might think of left-hand gestures, especially those that are cues or accents, in terms of how the hand might touch something that makes the desired sound. If the sound should be light and soft then the left hand might be more curved, fingers slightly spread, with the middle finger curved slightly lower than the others. The left hand is allowed to show tension where the right hand usually cannot. This is very useful to the conductor to show a sustained line or an increase in volume. The conductor might practice imagining using the left hand to touch different objects in different manners, for example, ringing an old-fashioned desk clerk's bell or touching the surface of a swimming pool to see how cold the water is. Left-hand gestures can be made with the palm facing the ensemble or the back of the hand facing the ensemble. Generally speaking, showing the ensemble the back of the hand will cause them to respond with a more aggressive, often louder sound. The palm of the hand is used for softer or more gentle gestures and sounds.

The left hand can be used to mirror the right hand in the basic pattern and style of the music. This is usually used at moments in the music that are of a loud and/or climactic nature. The conductor should be careful not to cross the hands when mirror conducting. It should be noted that when mirroring a 4/4 beat pattern, the left hand should move opposite the right hand on beats 2 and 3. The same idea is true of other beat patterns. There seems to be a temptation on the part of many conductors to overuse mirror conducting. Perhaps this is caused by conductors not really knowing what to do with the left hand. But the overuse of mirror conducting trains the ensemble not to look at the left hand if it always says the same thing as the right.

The left hand is very useful in the execution of cues. Because it does not hold a baton, it is more flexible in the type of cue that can be delivered. Two standard left-hand cue gestures are described here.

When cueing an individual or section that enters in a soft and/or delicate fashion, the conductor can use the following: bring the left hand into the conducting plane several beats prior to the cue, with the palm facing the ensemble place the fingers of the hand in a rounded "C" with the thumb and forefinger touching. Prepare the cue with the appropriate style prep beat, and on the ictus of the entrance gently pull the thumb and forefinger apart. This cue usually employs the elbow and wrist hinges.

A similar gesture with alteration can be used to cue a forte entrance or a large group of players. First, bring the left hand into the conducting plane early to attract the attention of the players. Next, with the palm facing the conductor, prepare the cue. Finally, on the ictus of the entrance, open the C-shape hand with a full stop created by the elbow hinge, no wrist break.

Any number of variations of these cues can be made with practice.

Exercise 5.45 ***First Suite in E flat, Intermezzo,*** Gustav Holst

Exercise 5.46 ***Brandenburg Concerto No. 2, mvt. 2,*** J. S. Bach

Exercise 5.47 *Sleepers Awake,* J. S. Bach

♩= 72

Exercise 5.48 *Cues*

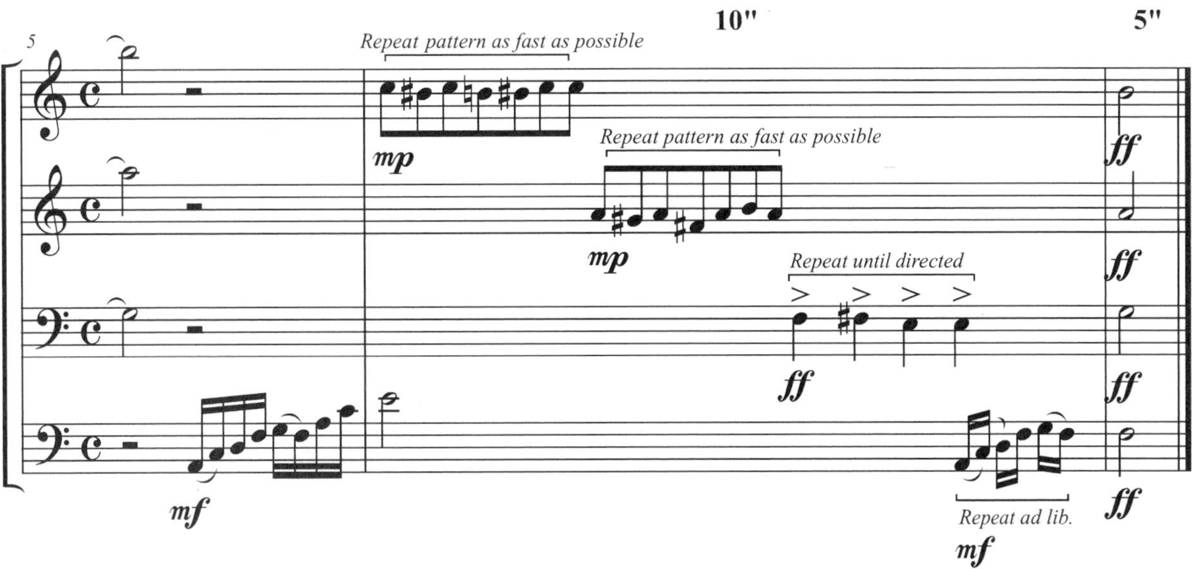

Exercise 5.49 *Cues*

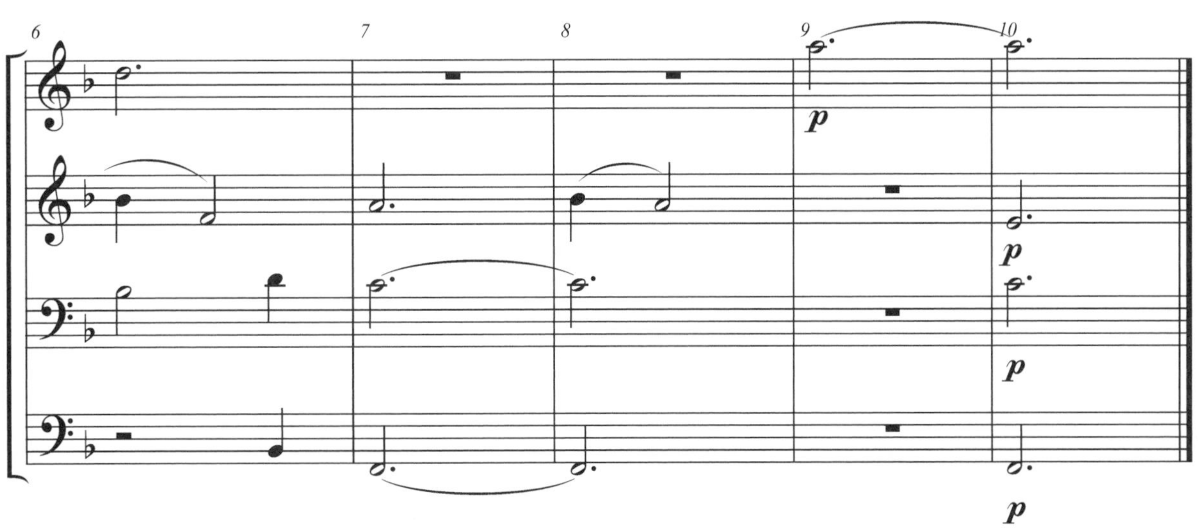

The left hand is also used to indicate dynamic changes. Used in conjunction with a changing size beat pattern, these indications can be very effective. The most commonly used left-hand gesture for dynamic change is a slow, smooth rise from the rest position to top of the conducting plane to indicate a crescendo and the opposite to effect a diminuendo. While most conductors can create this smooth motion using just the left hand, it will take much practice to do so while conducting a beat pattern with the right hand. The smooth and fluid up-and-down motion is essential for this gesture to be effective. The left hand is also used to indicate dynamic corrections that the conductor wishes the players to make. When wanting less volume from a section or player, the conductor brings the left hand up and, with fingers together, holds the left palm up to the player. If the conductor wants more volume he can do the same gesture with the back of the hand showing to the player.

Exercise 5.50 ***Overture in G Minor,*** Anton Bruckner

Exercise 5.51 ***A Toye,*** Giles Farnabye

These gestures have become almost universal to indicate that a player should be softer or louder and should need no verbal instruction.

As stated in Chapter 4, the left hand can assist with clarity of releases.

An important and advanced use of the left hand is to help shape the phrase. The left hand can show the ensemble the conductor's intent of phrase tension and release. A gesture that often works well to indicate phrase direction is to move the left hand and arm in a combined vertical and horizontal (almost diagonally) fashion from left to right across the body. Another such gesture is to slowly and smoothly turn the left hand in a rotating fashion as if turning from palm facing the ensemble to palm facing the conductor. This gesture works well to indicate an increase in tension in the music or a small crescendo.

The conductor who has full use of the left hand as an expressive tool is a much more effective and efficient communicator.

Exercise 5.52 ***Missa Papae Marcelli, "Kyrie,"*** Giovanni Pierluigi da Palestrina

Lento

1 2 3 4 5 6 7 8 9

mp

Exercise 5.53 ***Music for the Royal Fireworks, "Le Paix,"*** George Frideric Handel

Exercise 5.54 ***Chester,*** William Billings

NOTE

1. Green, Elizabeth. *The Modern Conductor.* Pearson Prentice Hall, Upper Saddle River, NJ, 2004.

CHAPTER 6

Expression in Conducting

Once a conductor has mastered the proper stance and basic patterns, he must begin the more difficult process of learning how to look like the music. Without this ability the communication between the conductor and the ensemble is limited to time keeping and verbal instructions. When considering the physical side of conducting, one should strive to make all gestures in the style of the music. This articulation of conducting gestures affects musical articulation, dynamics, cueing, and all other aspects of conducting save time keeping. Conducting becomes an art when the conductor is able to express the intent of the composer through gesture. While time keeping is an important part of this, it remains just one aspect of what the conductor must be able to do in order to lead an ensemble of musicians to an informed and musically rewarding performance.

FACIAL EXPRESSIONS

Facial expressions are the most important aspect of communication between a conductor and an ensemble. Our expressions often speak louder than our words or our gestures. As such, they must match the music or they negate our other communication.

The wind band–conducting pedagogue Allan McMurray[1] states that the eyes are the most important body part for the conductor because they reveal the soul. A major part of facial expression happens with the eyes and eyebrows, and gaining control of these is the first step to intentional facial expression. Practicing basic facial expressions in front of a mirror is essential to this development. By narrowing or widening the eyes and raising or squinting with the eyebrows, the conductor can express general feeling and style. To demonstrate this, stand in front of a mirror, with your left hand covering your mouth and chin. Try narrowing and widening your eyes and observe the change of expression of your face. Raise your eyebrows. Push your eyebrows toward the center of your nose in a squinting fashion. Each of these moves is very expressive and can communicate a mood without the aid of the hands, arms, or even the rest of your face.

The conductor should attempt to convey the following emotions/expressions using only the eyes and eyebrows:

Anger
Surprise
Joy
Apprehension
Determination
Elation

The next most important expressive part of the body is the mouth. The conductor can use the open or closed mouth as an aid in communicating a facial expression. Generally speaking, the open mouth communicates a softer, gentler mood and the closed mouth a more determined or louder one. This is probably because our mouths are open when we smile and closed when we frown. When using only the mouth, most conductors find it easier to express the more negative emotions such as anger or disgust. But it is possible to express happiness by focusing only on the mouth. Try this by starting with a deadpan, inexpressive face and slowly bring the corners of your mouth up into an open-mouthed smile. Watch your eyes while you do this. Even though you do not change your eyes, they appear to sparkle more and become brighter simply by changing your mouth. Stand in front of the mirror, again focusing this time on the mouth, trying not to change your eyes or eyebrows, and try to express the same emotions/expressions as above.

The combination of the mouth and eyes is a powerful communicative tool. Each of the expressions we have tried so far is enhanced by using both the mouth and the eyes. For example, try expressing surprise by opening and rounding your mouth, extending the length of your face by dropping your jaw, raising your eyebrows, and widening your eyes. This combination is much more effective than just the use of the eyes and eyebrows. Here is a simple guide to assist you in producing various expressions:

Expression	**Mouth**	**Eyebrows**	**Other**
Anger	Closed	Narrowed in a squint	
Surprise	Open	Raised	Wide eyes
Joy	Smiling	Raised	Open eyes
Apprehension	Open	Raised	Wide eyes
Determination	Lips together	Narrowed	Set jaw closed
Elation	(extension of expressions used for joy)		

Each of these expressions should be used to help the conductor express the music, and they should appear to be natural and spontaneous rather than practiced. Facial expressions cannot be constructed, practiced, and applied in specific measures of music. To do so lacks sincerity. Expression is not added on top of the music, it comes from the music itself. The conductor's own understanding of and feeling for the music must create the facial expressions. Honest facial expressions equate with the use of inflection in our voice. The exercises suggested above have two purposes: (1) to allow the conductor to truly get to know his face and how the face can be used to imitate mood/emotion and (2) to demonstrate how connected facial expressions are to our general body language and posture.

POSTURE AND BODY LANGUAGE

You may have noticed while practicing these expressions in front of the mirror that your posture changed naturally along with your facial expressions. The way in which a conductor holds the body can have a dramatic effect on the sound produced by an ensemble. In Chapter 3 a certain conducting stance was recommended. However, once the conductor feels comfortable on the podium he should vary this stance and posture according to the style of the music. The body posture and language used must aid the face and hands in communicating the style of the music to the ensemble.

The expressive body posture is most affected by the position of the shoulders; the position of the chest; the overall height of the conductor (not whether or not the person is short or tall, but whether or not the conductor uses the full height); the amount of flexibility in the knees, waist, and ankles; and the movement of the head.

The shoulders are much more malleable and easily positioned when not conducting than when beating a pattern. Three possible shoulder positions that are usable in conducting might include: (1) shoulders high and up (this might only be possible with elbows collapsed back and hands close together) (2) shoulders drooping and relaxed (certainly seems possible when elbows are collapsed and tucked into the body), and (3) shoulders back and neither drooped or up (this is the most used shoulder position in conducting).

The regular conducting position of the chest is up and out. When combined with the shoulders back, this is a commanding posture. It might best be achieved with relaxation by imagining that a string attached to the top of your head is being pulled taut upwards. This usually causes conductors to stand up tall, shoulders back, chest out and up and is the basic stance for conducting. The overall height of the conductor can be altered by relaxing or drawing tight this imaginary string. This action affects the position of the chest, usually causing the chest to drop and pull back as the string is relaxed and to rise and move forward as the string goes taut. The combination of the chest movement and overall height change can be useful to demonstrate different musical styles. The tall/chest up/head level/shoulders back position is used when music is of a martial, noble style and often at a forte dynamic. The lower body is also generally rigid in this stance. Conversely, the relaxed and low chest/shoulders collapsed/shorter stance is useful to demonstrate a relaxation in the music or a softer passage.

The flexibility of the waist, knees, and ankles also affects the body language communicated to the ensemble. In the normal conducting stance, all of these hinges are rigid, but most conductors regularly flex these hinges as part of their conducting body language. The waist hinge should mostly be used to rotate from left to right to address different sections of the ensemble. This rotation is preferable to turning the feet and entire body. The knees should remain flexible, but conductors should not bend at the knees to make their overall height change. This effect is best achieved by the upper body movements described above. The ankles allow the conductor to shift the body weight along the feet. This shifting is very useful. Generally speaking, shifting the weight forward and leaning toward the ensemble causes the ensemble members to intensify their sounds and/or get louder. Shifting the weight to the back of the feet and leaning away from the ensemble usually causes them to play lighter and/or softer.

Purposeful movement of the head seems to naturally accompany many facial expressions. When you practiced facial expressions in front of the mirror, you probably saw your head changing angles, your chin dropping, or felt your chin rising as your chest rose and you assumed your full height. These natural tendencies should not be hindered because they contribute to the overall facial expression that is projected to the ensemble.

HINGES

As discussed in Chapters 2 and 5, in order to change the style of the gesture, conductors make use of a number of joints or "hinges" along the arm and hands. These hinges include the shoulder, elbow, wrist, and fingers. By combining hinges or isolating the use of one hinge, the overall appearance of the hands and arms changes. The more hinges that are used, the more fluid and lyrical the style of gesture will be. In order to produce the most legato of gestures, a conductor might employ the shoulder, elbow, and wrist simultaneously. To produce a fast, staccato pattern, the conductor might use only the wrist or the fingers. The wrist is, perhaps, the most important hinge in expressive conducting. The elbow and shoulder hinges are often used primarily for time-keeping tasks.

Exercise 6.1 ***Chester,*** William Billings

COMBINING THE ELEMENTS

In order to express the music to the ensemble, the advanced conductor combines complete and natural control of the right- and left-hand conducting gestures with appropriate facial expressions, body language, and posture. This full package of gestures is what allows the conductor to "be the music" and to communicate style to the ensemble. It generally takes years of experience to be able to gain full control of one's gestures, and each of the elements must be practiced just as musicians practice scales and excerpts. Repetition of gestures is the road to familiarity and control of these gestures. It might be best to remember that all of these gestures are natural. Each of the facial expressions and body movements suggested in this chapter are a part of everyday life. They only begin to be difficult to produce when the conductor faces the task of conducting patterns, controlling the body, listening for and correcting player errors, and inspiring and controlling large groups of people. In order to accomplish all these things simultaneously, conductors must do all they can to make the predictable side of conducting easy, natural, and second nature to them. The unpredictable side—hearing/correcting errors and leading people—takes so much concentration that the technical aspects of conducting can consume only a small amount of the successful conductor's mental energy.

The conductor should practice the toolbox of gestures regularly. Even when experienced, you should practice facial expressions, body language, and control of the hands and arms. However, you should not take a musical score and identify places where you will automatically insert certain gestures or expressions. The automatic placement of an expression of joy or anger each time a work is played will make that expression meaningless to the ensemble over time and is as bad an error as giving no expression. The conductor, therefore must be able to draw from his gesture toolbox spontaneously in response to what he hears from the ensemble players and what the music demands. Bruno Walter, in his book *Of Music and Music*

Making[2] warns conductors not to put more expression into a work than they themselves feel about the work. This warning, when heeded, keeps us from becoming monotonous and repetitive in our conducting gestures. It keeps us conducting in the moment and conducting what we are hearing, not what is playing in our head. Most conductors are warned not to learn scores with recordings because in doing so we often hear that performance again rather than the performance of the ensemble in front of us. The same is true of gestures. Gestures cannot be assigned to specific moments in the score and then reproduced at the appropriate moment or the ensemble will learn not to watch and the performance and conductor will appear wooden.

Exercise 6.2 ***Carnival of the Animals, "The Swan,"*** Camille Saint-Saens

Exercise 6.3 *Old Comrades March,* Carl Teike

Exercise 6.4 *"Dance of the Sugar Plum Fairy," The Nutcracker,* Pyotr Ilyich Tchaikovsky

Exercise 6.5 *Overture to Die Meistersinger von Nürnberg,* Richard Wagner

Exercise 6.6 *Peter and the Wolf,* Sergei Prokofiev

PHRASAL CONDUCTING

Music is notated in measures and assigned meter as a manner of communicating rhythmic structure. Sometimes the music has a phrasal structure that does not consistently align with the assigned meter or barlines. In such cases the advanced conductor might modify the conducting pattern to match the phrase structure rather than the meter. This can only be done when the ensemble is secure in the rhythmic pulse and does not need the conductor to provide a steady pattern. For example, in Exercise 6.7 the conductor might abandon the three-beat meter once the pulse is established and conduct a pattern of four beats over four measures since the phrase structures are clearly in groups of four or multiples. This type of conducting shows the ensemble the phrase, not the beat.

Exercise 6.7 ***Greensleeves***

Another form of pattern modification is called "melding." This means that the conductor decides not to beat every beat of the pattern and instead shows only the beats that create the actual rhythmic of the work. In the following example, if the ensemble does not need the conductor to beat all beats, there is no musical reason to do so. Instead, the conductor might show the changes of rhythm and "meld" beats 1 and 2 together. Generally speaking, this melding fuses together two or more icti into a smooth gesture.

Example 6.1
Melding.

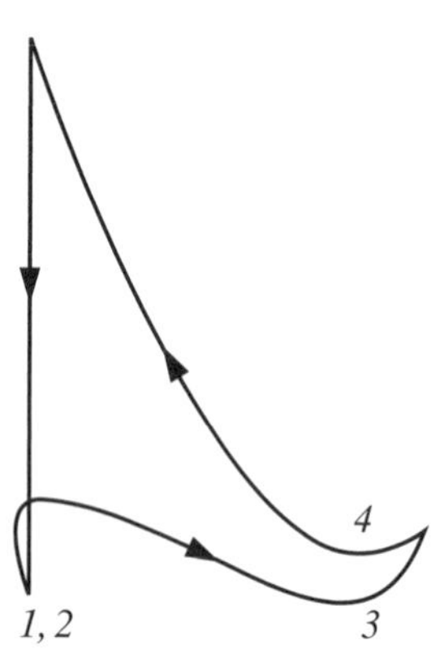

Exercise 6.8 *Melding Exercise*

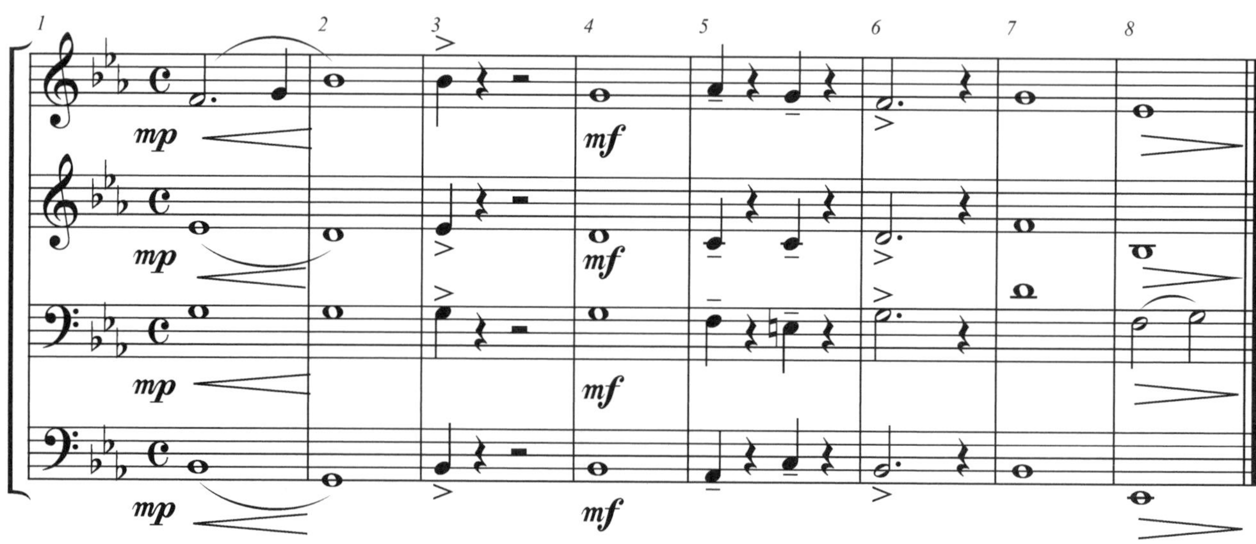

The conductor might also choose to modify the pattern by de-emphasizing certain icti of the pattern. This device is usually used to emphasize a certain measure or movement within a measure. It is very useful in conducting a work in three for the conductor to emphasize beat 1 of the pattern and de-emphasize beats 2 and 3 (such as in a waltz).

Finally, the advanced conductor knows that once the ensemble no longer needs the beat pattern, it can be abandoned in favor of more expressive gestures. There is no reason to continue beating a pattern in a monotonous fashion if the ensemble does not need it. To do so simply trains members not to watch the conductor. The left hand can be used to conduct accents, phrases, entrances cues, etc. without the right hand in a pattern at all. This type of conducting frees the conductor to focus completely on being the music and showing the style of the music to the ensemble.

The following exercises combine many of the technical and musical problems discussed throughout the text.

Exercise 6.9 *Comprehensive Exercise 1*

♩= 60

♩= 80

accel.

♩= 120

rit.

Exercise 6.10 ***Comprehensive Exercise 2***

Canzon, Samuel Scheidt
𝅗𝅥 = 88
♩ = 104
In 1
♩ = 110
p
mp
mf
f
ff

Exercise 6.11 *Comprehensive Exercise Opera Excerpts*

The Magic Flute, Mozart

1 **Adagio** 2 3 3 4 5 *Ten.*

ff *p*

ff *Ten.* *p*

ff *Ten.* *p*

ff *Ten.* *p*

♩= 66 *Don Giovanni, Mozart*

6 7 8 9 *rit.* 10 11

mp

rit. *mp*

rit. *mp*

rit. *mp*

♩= 42
Madame Butterfly, Puccini
mf
mp
mp
mp

Tempo di valse
Die Fledermaus, Strauss
pp
cresc. e accel.molto
pp
cresc. e accel.molto
pp
cresc. e accel.molto
pp
cresc. e accel.molto

rit.
f
rit.
rit.
f
rit.
rit.
f
rit.
rit.
f
rit.

William Tell Overture, Rossini
♩= 132
28
29
30
31
32
33
34
f

35
36
37
38
39
40
41
42
f
f
f

43
44
45
46

Nessun Dorma, Puccini

Exercise 6.12 *Comprehensive Exercise*

Just Before the Battle Mother

Drunken Sailor

12
13
14
15
mp
mf
f
ten.
Divinum Mysterium
16
17
18
19
p
20
21
3"
22
6"
23
6"
Rpt. as fast as possible
as directed
Directed

NOTES

1. Allan McMurray is Director of Bands at the University of Colorado at Boulder.
2. Walter, Bruno. *Of Music and Music Making.* W.W. Norton, New York, 1961.

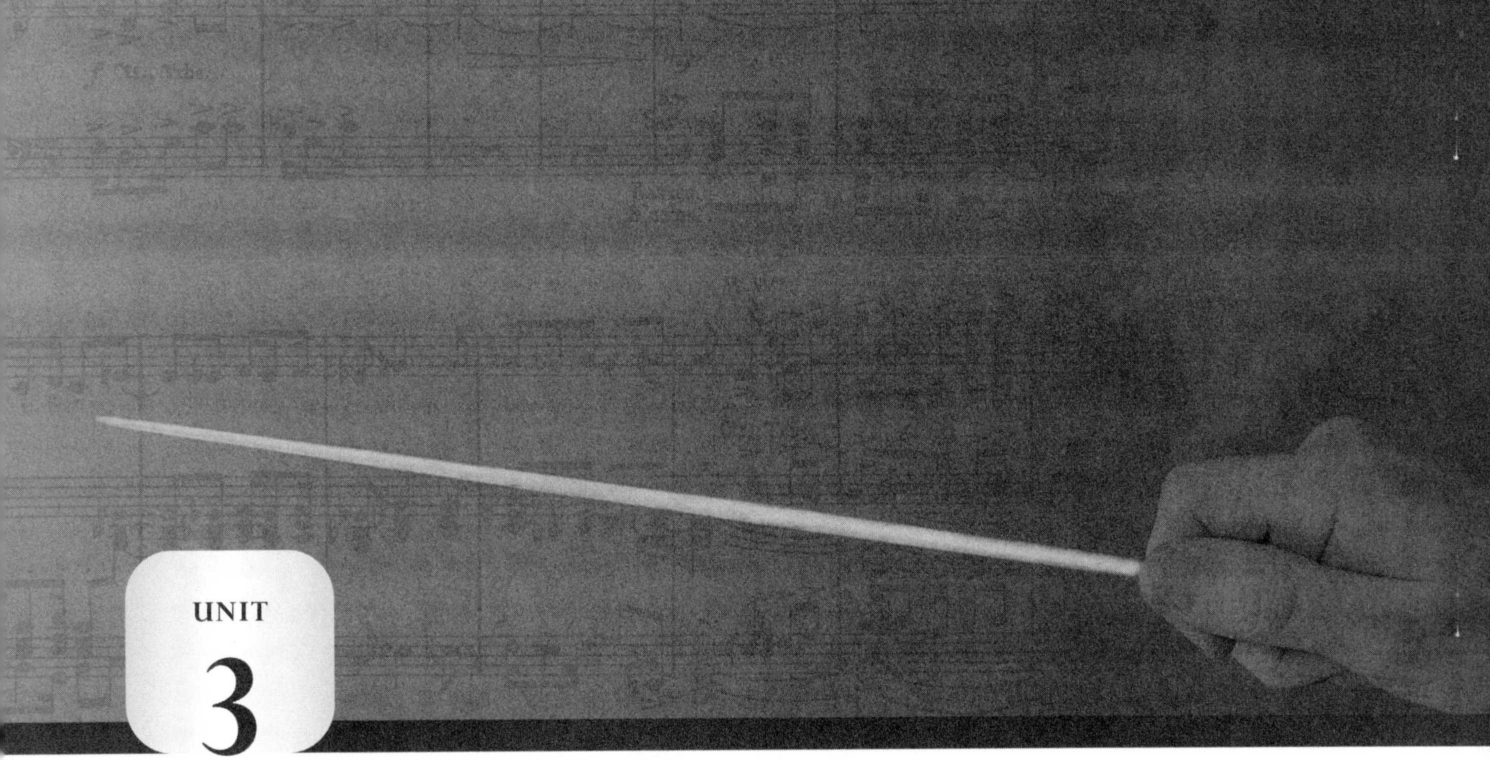

UNIT 3

Analysis *and* Interpretation

CHAPTER

7

Score Study

Why do conductors study scores? What does it mean to "study" a score?

The first question has some definite answers. The second is different for each conductor based upon his abilities and knowledge. Most importantly, conductors study scores in order to give an informed performance of a work. Since the players naturally look to the conductor to provide the interpretation of the work, he must base that interpretation upon knowledge, not intuition.

By studying the score the conductor can identify at least the following:

1. The construction and compositional craft of the work.
2. The technical aspects of conducting the music.
3. A prediction of technical difficulties that lie in store for the players.
4. Discrepancies between the score and the parts.

Conductors also study scores to devise rehearsal plans. All of these reasons cause the conductor to spend a great deal of time with the score prior to conducting it with an ensemble. In fact, the conductor spends much more time studying the score than rehearsing or performing it.

TYPES OF SCORES

When a conductor first opens a score, he must determine if the score is a concert pitch score or a transposed score. In most cases the score will be transposed, and this can be determined by looking at the key signatures of the individual parts. If they are different across the score, it is a transposed score. Unfortunately, it is not easy to identify a concert score. Generally speaking, the score is a concert score if all parts have the same key signature. However, many contemporary scores might appear this way and make use of accidentals throughout to create the appropriate transpositions. This is more unusual, but the conductor must be aware of this possibility. In most such cases there is no key signature.

Scores are also either full scores or condensed scores. A full score is the most useful to the conductor because it shows every part of the ensemble each measure of the work. A modified version of the full score is the "French score." In this type of score (see Example 7.4), long rests for instruments are not indicated. They are replaced with blank space, but staff space, is still allocated to them.

The condensed score is essentially a reduction of the instrumentation to the essential lines of the work. If a work only has four parts that are doubled throughout the ensemble, the score would consist of those four parts. Sometimes the lines are labeled as instruments add and drop off the lines, but often there is no indication which instruments play which lines. Often percussion parts are left off the condensed score entirely. Condensed scores are almost always concert pitch scores.

Aleatoric music is often written in an iconic score. Such scores usually have a key to indicate to the performers and conductor what the icons mean.

CLEFS AND TRANSPOSITIONS

The conductor must be able to read C, G, and F clefs with equal fluency. There is a C clef that can be used for each line and space of the staff. The clef identifies middle C. The two most commonly used C clefs for an instrumental conductor are the alto clef, which identifies the third line as middle C, and the tenor clef, which places middle C as the fourth line of the staff. The conductor should realize that these clefs exist primarily to avoid writing ledger lines and make parts easier to read.

The F clef is also called the bass clef, and the G clef is referred to as the treble clef. Most students of conducting will already be familiar with these clefs.

The conductor will encounter two types of transposition problems: (1) learning to easily transpose to concert pitch the written notes of many instruments and (2) learning to transpose to concert pitch the written notes of transposing instruments that are also playing a transposed part themselves. The first problem has to do with the overtone series of the modern instruments. For example, B-flat clarinet parts are written a major second higher than their sounding pitch. In the traditional band and orchestra, the clarinet, saxophone, trumpet, and horn parts are all transposing wind instruments. The student should memorize the transposition chart below to learn these transposition rules. The conductor must develop the ability to read numerous transpositions simultaneously in order to read a band or orchestral score.

The second problem is hard for many conductors to understand. It usually only comes up in older scores and is most common in orchestral music. Because many of the instruments were still in developmental stages until about the beginning of the twentieth century, wind instrument keys were not generally standardized. Composers might write for a particular instrument, say horn, pitched in a particular key rather than always writing for horn in F, as a composer would do today. For example, many Classical and Romantic era horn parts are written for C, B-flat, D, or E-flat horn. Today, the player will play these parts on an F horn and transpose the part themselves so that the appropriate concert pitch comes out of the instrument. Therefore, the contemporary horn player using an F horn playing a horn part written for E-flat horn will transpose all pitches down a major second so that the

Example 7.1 Full band score, concert, *Variants on a Mediaeval Tune*, Norman Dello Joio.

Example 7.2 Full orchestra score, transposed, *La Mer*, Claude Debussy.
(Used with permission, Dover Publications, Inc., New York. "Three Great Orchestral Works" by Claude Debussy.)

Example 7.3 Full band score, transposed, *Blue Shades*, Frank Ticheli.
(Courtesy of www.ManhattanBeachMusic.com)

Example 7.4 French score, *Pittsburgh Overture*, Krzysztof Penderecki.

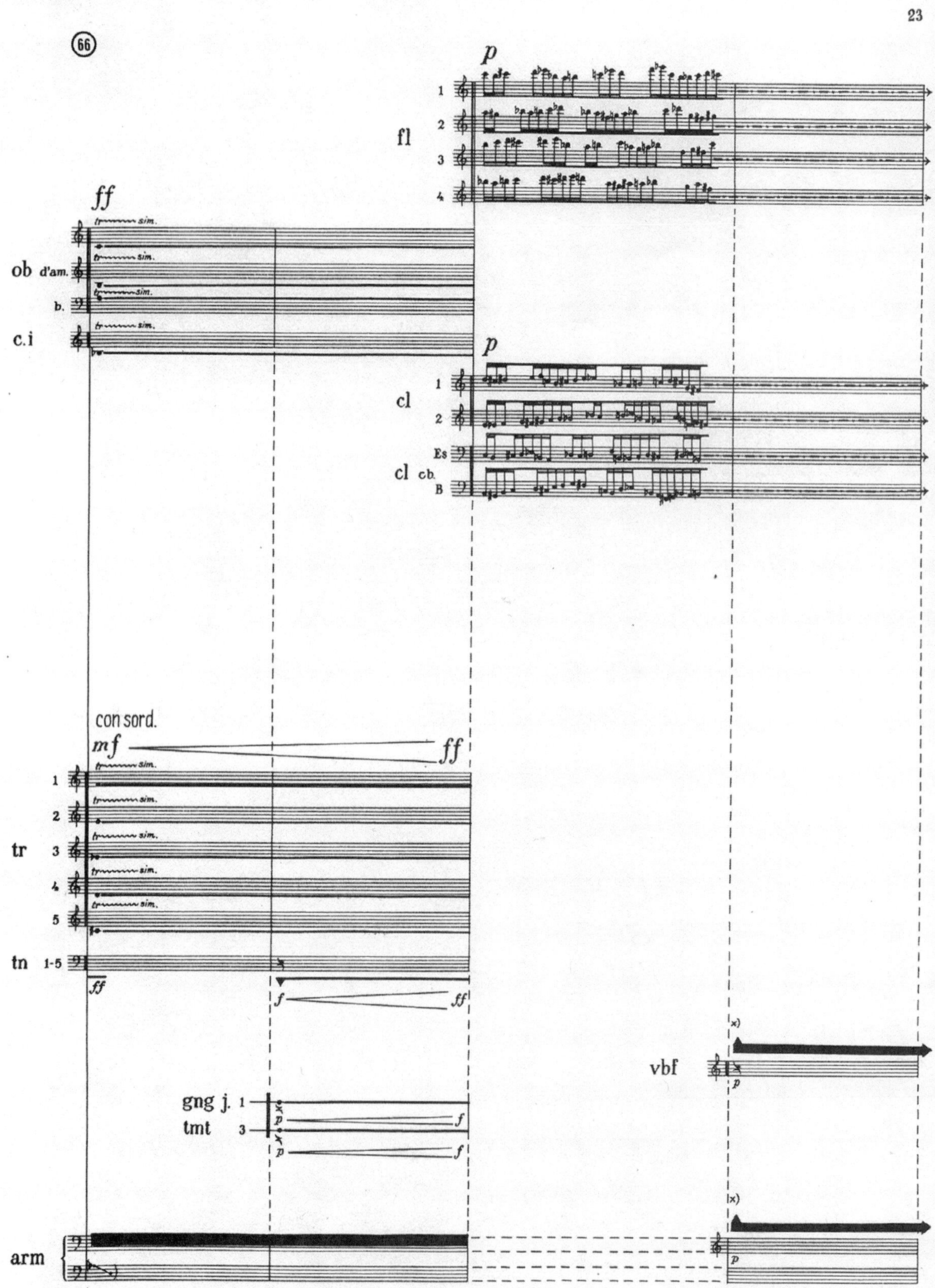

Example 7.5 Condensed score, Suite of Old American Dances, Robert Russell Bennett.

Example 7.6 Aleatoric *Score, Symphony No. 1,* Daniel Bukvich

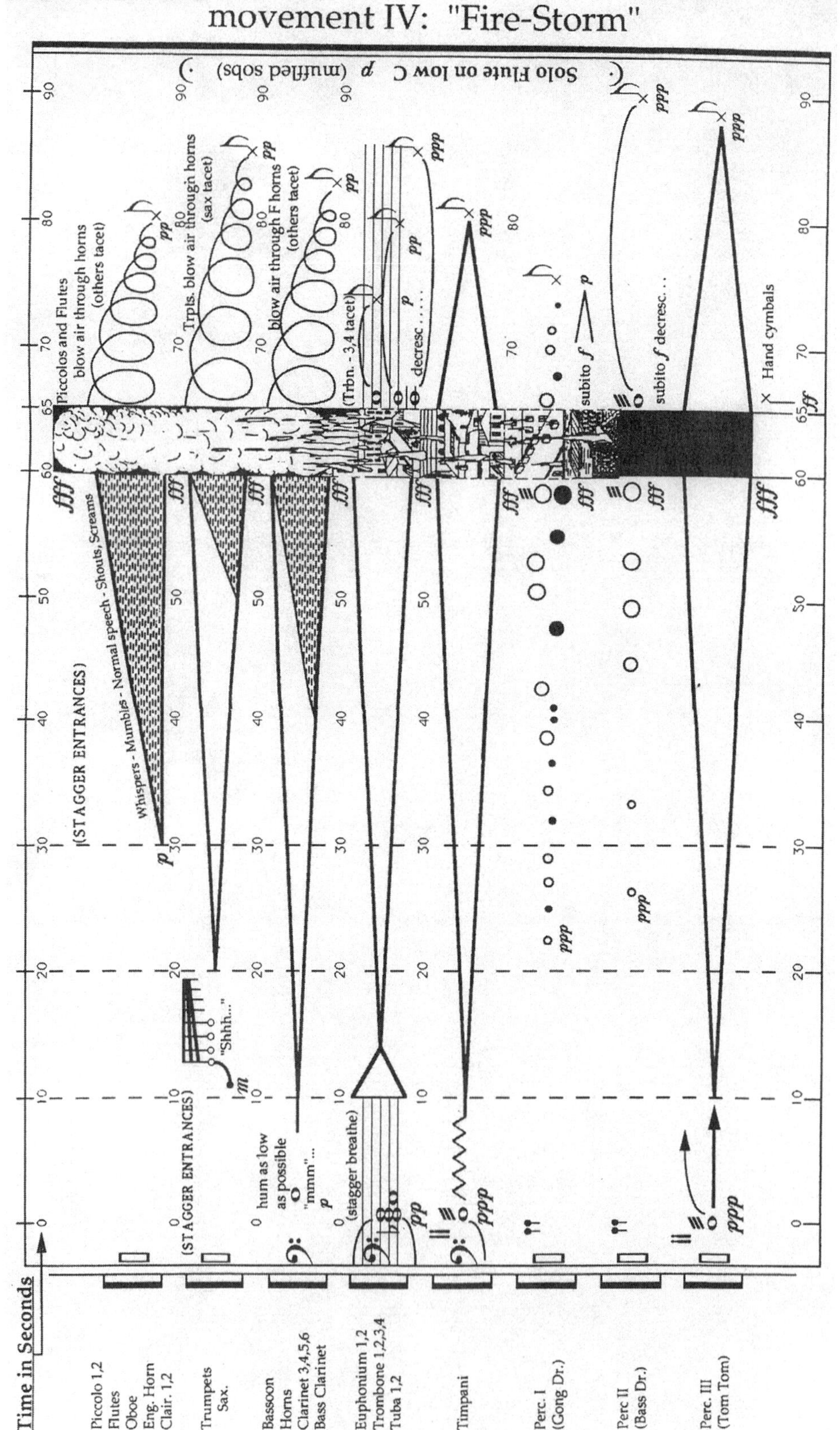

Example 7.7
Clefs (middle C is indicated in each clef).

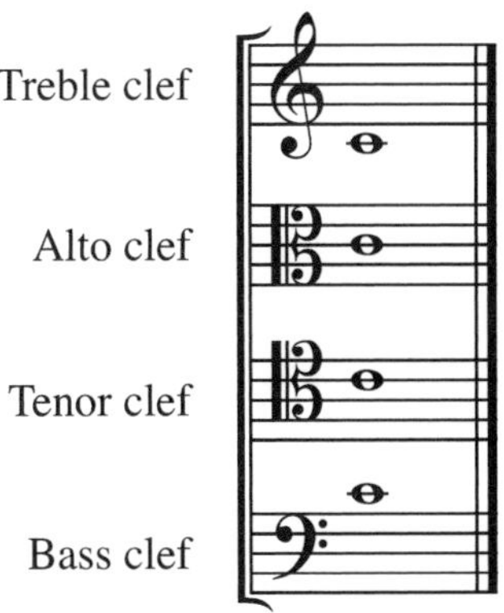

sounding pitch comes out right. The sounding pitch for an F horn is a perfect fifth lower than written. The combination of these two transpositions causes the conductor to read the E-flat horn part down a major sixth in order to find the correct sounding note. This is common in orchestral music for horn and trumpet and for band music of the first half of the twentieth century for horn. These players are taught to read multiple transpositions as easily as they read at pitch.

The student should memorize the transposition chart in Example 7.8.

SCORE STUDY

In working with a new score, the conductor should work from a big picture understanding of the score to specifics, and then back to the big picture., i.e., introduction/overview, analysis, synthesis.

In the introduction stage the conductor is aiming to gain an overall understanding of the work in order to reach a general understanding of the sound of the work in his head. We begin this overview process with the title page because it often tells us many important things about the work, such as the form, key, and style. Take, for example, the title "Variants on a Mediaeval Tune"[1] by Norman Dello Joio. By simply reading the title we can make the following assumptions (these may be proved wrong later but are a good starting place): the form of the work is theme and variations, the form of the theme might be AB (since most variation themes are two-part), the work might be modal since the tune is from the Middle Ages, and the work is contemporary because of the name of the composer. These all go a long way in helping us begin the second phase of our score study analysis. Other titles might place a work historically, tell its actual key, place it in the development of a composer (by its opus number), suggest key relationships in various movements, or suggest relationships to other works by the composer. For example, the title "Symphony No. 39 in E-flat" by Wolfgang Amadeus Mozart suggests the following: the work is in four movements—the key of movements 1 and 4 is E-flat, movement 2 might be in c minor or A-flat, movement 3 might begin in B-flat. The first movement is

Example 7-8 Transposition chart.

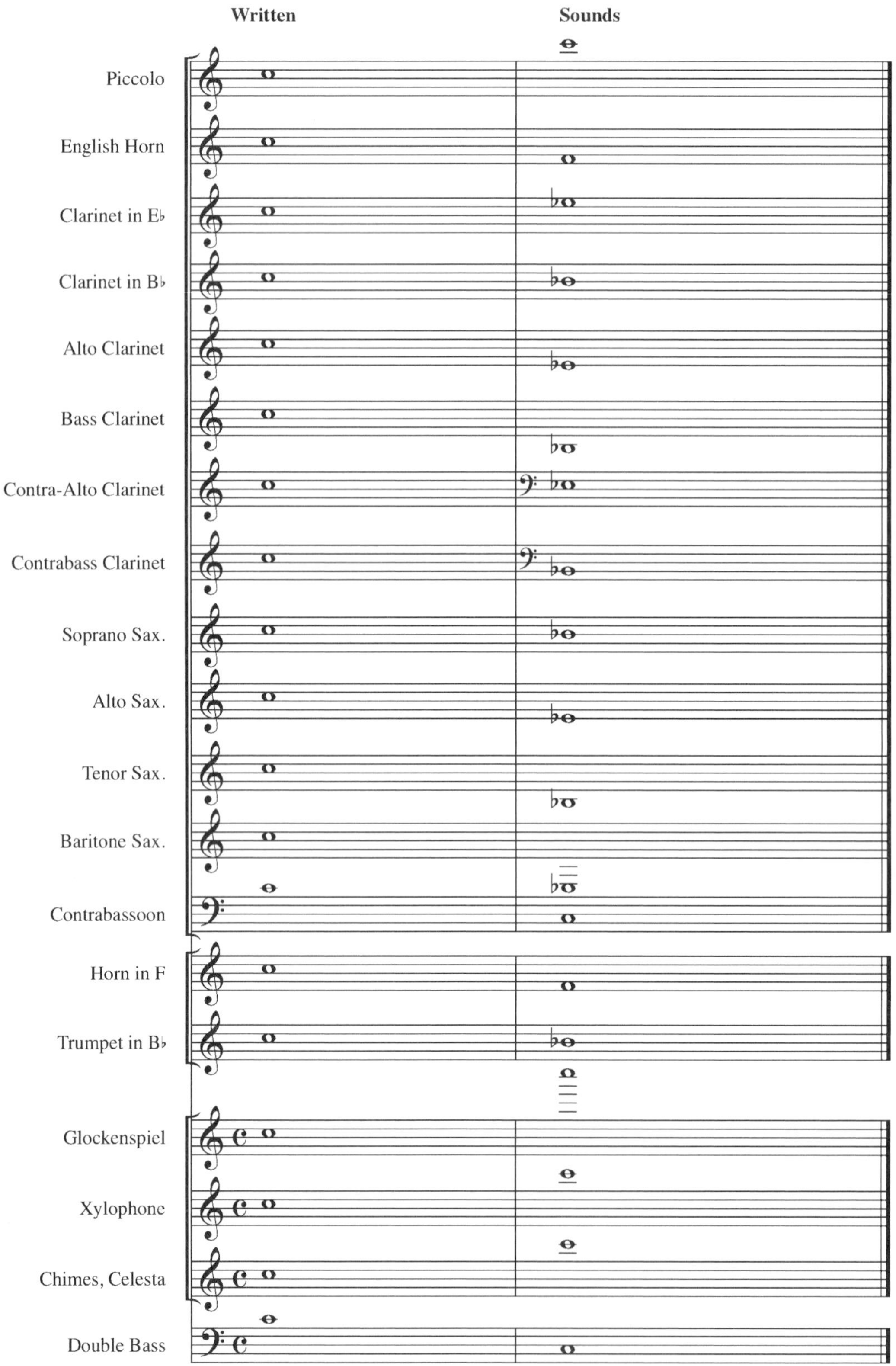

probably a sonata form, the second a song form, the third a minuet and trio, and the fourth either a sonata or a rondo form. The work is a mature work by Mozart because of its number. It is scored for strings and winds in pairs because that was the dominant type of instrumentation of the period. Chances are that the work will have two primary themes in the sonata forms. All of this is predictable simply from the work's title and by making use of the music theory and history that we all have learned about the Classical era. The conductor uses this storehouse of knowledge to help predict what might be proven true or false later in the analysis of the score.

The overview section of score study should also provide the conductor with information about the composer, arranger, and/or editor. The composer's name can provide clues to the sound of the work and to its overall style. For example, the composer William Schuman wrote several works for band in the twentieth century. Once his style traits have been learned, the conductor can look at another work, predicting that those might appear again. The work "George Washington Bridge"[2] for band by Schuman is a good example. When opening this score for the first time, the conductor should consider Schuman's important compositional traits. Schuman wrote works that were usually bitonal or tritonal in nature and often used quartal harmonies. These polytonalities are usually presented a major second or perfect fourth apart. Schuman used percussion outbursts to delineate form. He contrasted families of instruments against each other to create tone color changes. All of these traits can be used by the conductor to aid the beginning of the analysis process. Once the conductor knows the style traits of a composer, analysis becomes a matter of prediction and proof, proving predictions either correct or wrong.

The title page can also provide the conductor with information on the instrumentation required to perform the work. It allows the conductor to discover any unusual instruments that might not ordinarily be part of the ensemble—assuming that the conductor knows the standard instrumentation of the orchestra and symphonic band. The conductor will also determine from the first page the type of score: full or condensed, concert or transposed.

In addition to the information provided on the title page, the overview process should provide the conductor a general idea of the following:

1. Tempo or tempi of the work.
2. Overall style of the work: lyrical? marcato? etc.
3. Overall texture: Full ensemble throughout? Chamber music or solo sections? Contrasting in nature?
4. Dominant timbre of the work: Not all band or orchestral works should sound the same in terms of timbre, especially twentieth-century music.
5. Style or type of ending.
6. Number of movements.
7. Conducting challenges.

The hard work of score study takes place in the analysis phase. The goal of this study time is to gain an intimate knowledge of the construction of the work. The conductor should begin the analysis by determining the form of the work. Knowing the form can often provide clues to key and phrase structures, or even tempo. The conductor must first determine whether the work is in a standard form. If not, assign letters (A,B,C, etc.) to each of the major sections or melodies. To identify form, try using the markings that the editor or composer provided. Often the existence of double bars, key changes, repeat signs, measure numbers, or total numbers of measures can help identify the form. Or look at the entrance and exit of instruments, especially percussion. Climaxes are often punctuated by percussion entrances, and the conductor can sometimes develop an understanding of the form by looking at the instrumentation changes. Create a flow chart like in Example 7.9 listing the major sections and numbers of measures of the work. This visual aid will come in handy later when the conductor identifies climaxes and phrase structure. Generally, the use of repetition and contrast creates form in a work.

Once the form is determined, the conductor should study the melody. Identifying the form usually tells the conductor how many distinct melodies the work possesses because form is created by the repetition and contrast of ideas. The conductor should be able to determine from this whether or not the melodies are developmental in style, imitative in nature, germinal (based upon a specific small motif), or variations. He should also identify on the form chart where the melodic structure is lyrical, marcato, soaring, or make use of other descriptive words. Next, the conductor should determine whether or not the melodies are related to one another. Do all melodies grow from one main idea? Are all melodies of a particular style or type? Do the melodies all use some rhythmic motive or interval? Finally, the conductor should identify the intervallic structure and range of the melodies. What intervals appear to be most important? Are those intervals used in other ways? Are the intervals connected to the key structure or harmonic structure of the work?

When studying the harmonic structure of the work the conductor should first ask: "Is the work harmonic, is it vertical in nature, is it polyphonic, or is it linear?" If the work is truly harmonic, the conductor must determine if it uses bitonal, polytonal, quartal, or traditional harmonies. Also, is this harmonic structure related in

Example 7.9
Flowchart.

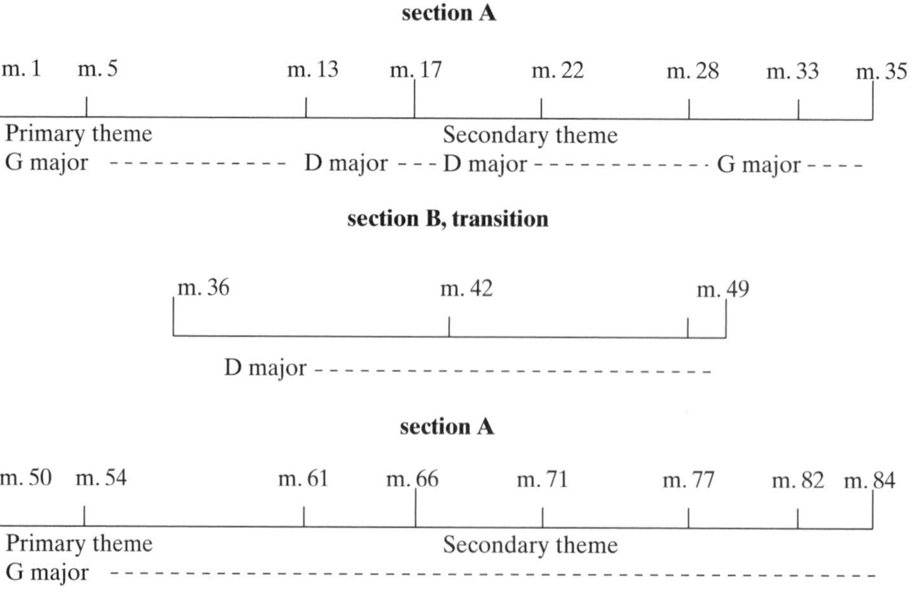

any manner to the important intervals of the melodies? Taking our example of "George Washington Bridge" again, the important melodic intervals are the M2 and P4, and those are also the important bitonalities used harmonically. It is important in studying harmonic structure for the conductor to look at the score with eyes of the time in which the score was written. In so doing the conductor will more easily see things that might have been remarkable at the time of writing which are commonplace today. For example, if we were to hear a work by Mozart end on a tonic chord with an added sixth and ninth, that would have been remarkable. But in a contemporary work such an ending chord is commonplace and may not have any significant meaning to the work. Where composers stray from the predictable, especially in harmonies, is where the conductor should pay closest attention.

Next, the conductor studies closely the rhythmic structures of the work, including tempo and rubato. The conductor should determine if the work contains a motivic rhythm that is important in the style of the work or that is developed throughout the work. The conductor should note where the composer uses tempo changes and rubato. Often these are used to help delineate the form for the listener.

In the analysis process the conductor should also determine the timbre of the work. This is created by the instrumentation and texture of the scoring. In contemporary scores the timbre is often the most important musical element of the work. Generally speaking, the conductor should determine (1) if timbre is an important element, or if the composer has written a work that should be played with a traditional orchestral or band sound, and (2) whether or not timbral changes occur in relation to the other structural elements of the work.

The conductor will be greatly aided by doing a linear analysis of the work in addition to the harmonic and formal analyses. This linear analysis helps the conductor identify tension and relaxation points of phrases, important climaxes, and the truly important pitches within a melodic line. Exmple 7.10 demonstrates this concept. For further instruction on linear analysis, the reader is referred to Gerald Warfield's excellent *Layer Analysis: a Primer of Elementary Tonal Structures.*[3]

Finally, in the analysis portion of score study, the conductor must identify the "compositional glue" of the work. What element or elements tie the work together? Is an interval of primary importance as a compositional device—is it timbre, form, or something else? What aspect of the composition is the root idea of the work?

Example 7.10 Linear analysis.

Linear Analysis, m. 17-24, mvt. 2, Symphony No. 35, Mozart

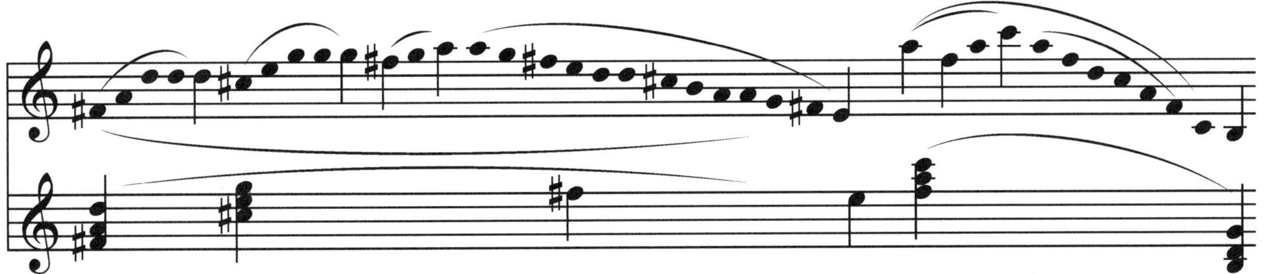

Not as part of the actual analysis of the work, but as part of the research about the score, the conductor should also identify and research performance practice of ornaments, rubato, and articulations that appear in the score. These items are often bound to the style of the work or to a particular historical period in music. The historically accurate production of a trill, turn, or articulation will be important to the overall effectiveness of the work.

Once the analysis of the score is finished the conductor should identify passages that might be problematic to the performers in a technical sense. Of course, these predictions are based upon one's knowledge of the instruments and experience in conducting. These predictions will aid the conductor in creating a rehearsal plan for the work.

"The whole duty of a conductor is comprised in his ability to indicate the right tempo."[4] Interpreting the score is one of the most important of conductor tasks and is the place where the conductor synthesizes all that he has learned about the work. The reason that conductors analyze scores is to provide an informed interpretation that represents the composer's intent.

Interpretation is the adjustment of the musical elements of a work to enhance the energies of the work. The following lend themselves to interpretation: tempo, rubato, timbre, climaxes, phrase tension/relaxation points, ornaments, fermata, articulations, silences, relative dynamic structures, general style of the work, and lines/parts to emphasize. Pitches, rhythms (in most cases except jazz), harmonies, and instrumentation are generally not to be altered. The notable exceptions are the interpretation of dotted rhythms and jazz rhythms.

The conductor must use his analysis to make decisions about the interpretive items listed above. The most important interpretive item might be tempo. Writers on conducting since Richard Wagner have stated that this is the most important and sometimes the only task of the conductor—getting the right tempo. In order to accomplish this, a conductor must take into consideration the tempo markings (in the absence of metronome markings) of the composer and what they meant at the time of the composition. For example, it is generally believed that the term "Allegro" is performed within a faster range of tempi today than during the mid-1800s. The conductor might consult old music encyclopedia to get an idea of the relative speed of tempo terminology. Erich Leinsdorf's book *The Composer's Advocate*[5] contains excellent sections on how a conductor goes about making tempo decisions.

Experienced performers realize that many markings in the score are relative and change based upon the composer being played. For example, a sforzando in a score by Haydn will be a very different sound than the same marking in a work by Wagner. The same is true of articulation and ornaments. The problem that performers and conductors face is figuring out when they are looking at a "traditional" notation versus a specific notation. Knowing musical traditions in different time/style periods will assist the conductor in determining where rubato is appropriate, what type of ornaments to use, and the general weight and strength of certain articulation markings. The analysis itself should indicate to the conductor which lines/parts to emphasize where and where the primary climaxes of the work are to be found.

Phrasing is a matter closely tied to form and rhythmic structure and is, perhaps, the most interpretive of items. Donald Barra, in his book *The Dynamic Performance,* [6] describes phrasing as "a purposeful motion toward and away from specific points of reference. Anything that draws attention toward one tone and away from another helps determine phrasing." The conductor should base his phrasing interpretations upon the linear analysis. All works have certain pitches that are destination points. Identifying these pitches and resolution points helps form the phrasing. However, if the work is harmonic in nature, the conductor must also consider the harmonic structure as well as the melodic contour in order to properly phrase a work.

The question of where interpretation becomes inappropriate manipulation is an important issue. The conductor cannot add or revise the score simply because he thinks it sounds good to do so. Ritards, for example, cannot be added unless there is a musical reason to do so. All interpretations to the score must be backed up by a reason discovered in the analysis of the work and/or musical traditions.

At the rehearsals the conductor should present the analysis and interpretation to the ensemble—not necessarily in a formal fashion, but it is important that the players learn some of the reasons why interpretative decisions are made. This will help them in their own interpretations of solo lines and also in remembering the conductor's directions.

REHEARSAL PLANNING

Planning a work's rehearsals mirrors score study in that the conductor usually gives the ensemble an overview of the work via a read-through, follows this with intensive rehearsal of specific passages, and finally puts the work back together to synthesize the piece into a whole.

The goal of the read-through is to provide the players with an overview of the entire work. From this they should gain an understanding of the style of the work and an idea of how technically challenging it will be for them as individuals. The conductor should focus the read-through on articulation and rhythm. If the ensemble plays these elements correctly, the players will gain a true idea of the style work. It is unlikely that the ensemble will be successful in playing straight through a work without having to stop. The conductor should identify in advance "regrouping" places where he purposefully stops in the reading to point out things to come and general problems that have occurred and to allow the players to refocus their thoughts.

The subsequent rehearsals should be planned but must be flexible in nature. Each rehearsal can best be planned by examining the successes and failures of the preceding rehearsal and then addressing those problems. One way to do this is to give assignments at the end of each rehearsal. Conductors often forget to do this, assuming that the players hear the same errors that they do. This is not the case. At the end of each rehearsal the conductor should identify specific sections of the work that players need to practice individually and why they should practice them.

Following each rehearsal the conductor should do a postrehearsal study of the score to identify sections that need to be rehearsed at the next meeting. This is most successful if the rehearsal is taped and the conductor can review the ensemble's performance.

MARKING THE SCORE

The conductor actually is best served using two scores for each work: a rehearsal study score and a performance score. The study score is marked for analysis purposes, and the performance score is marked for musical performances purposes. The study score might contain markings in different colors that remind the conductor of phrasings, climaxes, important lines that must be brought out, and actual theoretical analysis items. The performance score should be marked in pencil since each performance of the work will probably require different markings based upon different players. The performance score markings are usually reminders to the conductor of cueings, tempo modifications, and places where different players need the conductor's assistance.

NOTES

1. Dello Joio, Norman. "Variants on a Mediaeval Tune."
2. Schuman, William. "George Washington Bridge."
3. Warfield, Gerald. *Layer Analysis: a Primer of Elementary Tonal Structures*. Longman, New York, 1976.
4. Wagner, Richard. *On Conducting*. Dover Publications, Inc., New York, 1989.
5. Leinsdorf, Erich. *The Composer's Advocate*. Yale University Press, New Haven, CT, 1981.
6. Barra, Donald. *The Dynamic Performance*. Prentice Hall, Inc., Englewood Cliffs, NJ, 1983.

CHAPTER 8

Sample Score Analyses

In Chapter 7 you learned how to analyze scores for interpretation. This chapter provides two samples of analyzed scores using the method outlined in Chapter 7. In order to fully understand this chapter, you will need full scores for the following two works: *Symphony No. 35, KV 385*, movement 2, Wolfgang Amadeus Mozart, and *First Suite in E-flat*, movement 1, Gustav Holst. These two works have been chosen for analysis because they are readily available in almost any college/university music and band libraries.

Most analyses contain brief biographical information about the composers. However, these two composers are so well known that such an inclusion seems unnecessary for the purposes of this text.

SYMPHONY NO. 35, KV 385, ANDANTE, WOLFGANG AMADEUS MOZART

OVERVIEW

To begin to gain an overview understanding of the second movement of this symphony, you must start with the title page of the symphony itself. As suggested in Chapter 7, it is best to work from the "big picture" to specifics when first learning a score. The title page of the work provides a wealth of information about the piece, and from it we can make many predictions about the second movement itself before even seeing the score to the second movement.

Much of the history of the work can be discerned or researched from the title alone. The title *Symphony No. 35* tells us that Mozart had written at least thirty-four other symphonies, and this indicates that the work was a mature work. Because the title page also includes the indication "K.V. 385" we can place the work in a particular time period of Mozart's life. "K.V." refers to a numbering system devised by Dr. Ludwig Köchel and published in a catalog in 1862. The catalog arranges Mozart's more than 600 works approximately in the order in which he wrote them. In 1937 Alfred Einstein published a revised version of the Köchel catalog based upon more current research. The number 385 places the work in the last ten years of Mozart's life. In fact, upon examination of the autograph score we find that Mozart dated the first movement of the work July 1782. Much has been written about this particular symphony, and it is easy to find even more specific information about the dates of the other movements from Mozart's letters to his father, Leopold Mozart. This is because the commissioning of the work was closely related to Leopold Mozart. The work is subtitled "the Haffner Symphony," named in honor of the Haffner family, a well-to-do family in Salzburg for whom Mozart the younger had previously written a work for the wedding of Haffner's daughter, Elizabeth, to Franz Spath in July of 1776. The work had so pleased the family that Leopold Mozart convinced them to commission the new work for the ceremony of the ennoblement of Siegmund Haffner in 1782. Wolfgang Mozart wrote the work in installments, as fast as he could manage given all the other things he was working on. The complete work was sent to Salzburg on August 7, 1782, and was not a symphony. The piece was originally another serenade and was in six movements. The current *Symphony No. 35* is in four movements, including an Allegro, Andante, Minuet-Trio, and Presto. The original serenade included a second Minuet-Trio and a march. In the spring of 1783 Mozart presented one of his all-Mozart concerts in Vienna and reworked the Haffner serenade into the *Symphony No. 35*. He added two flutes and two clarinets, cut the second Minuet-Trio and the march, and presented the work as a symphony on March 3, 1783, with the emperor present.

While not all of this information can be obtained by simply looking at the title page of the symphony, the conductor should ask himself questions concerning origin, premiere, purpose of the work with each new score, the clues on the title page lead, in this case, quickly to very specific information.

The title page also gives clues about the key of the movements. The conductor can tell quickly from the title page that the primary key of the symphony is D major. Given rudimentary knowledge gained in any college music theory and history course sequence, the conductor can predict that the key of the second movement (the one that we are most interested in here) will be one of the following: G major, d minor, or b minor. These are the traditional keys of the second movement of a four-movement Classical era symphony in D major. Upon examination of the first page of the second movement, we find that the key is, in fact, G major just as predicted.

The form of the second movement can also be predicted based upon the title page of the work. Since the work is a Classical symphony, we can predict that it will be in a four-movement form, with the second movement being slower in tempo and more relaxed in style than the other three. Second movements of symphonies of this time period tend to be in one of the following forms: sonata, sonatina, ABA, or song form. Though it will take a bit of analysis work, the conductor will discover that this second movement is a sonatina.

The title page of the symphony also tells the conductor which clefs and instrument transpositions will be used in the work. In this case all four primary clefs are used in the work, and the conductor will need to be able to easily transpose horn in D, horn in G, and clarinet in A.

The title page shows the instrumentation of the work, which in this case is standard for the time period, including pairs of winds and traditional string complement.

The first page of the second movement gives the conductor more clues and items for research. Of immediate interest is the relationship between the title of the movement, "Andante," and the meter, 2/4. Without previous knowledge of traditions of the time or research into use of meters in the Classical era, the inexperienced conductor might attempt to play this work twice as fast as it should actually go. The work is actually in four beats per measure at a walking tempo.

Simply flipping through the score of the second movement, the conductor should observe that further research is required into the performance of the ornaments, the articulations, and the repeat signs. The lack of gradual dynamic changes and Mozart's use of only subito dynamic indications also deserves attention and consideration.

The conductor should also notice that the horn transposition has changed from the first movement.

The texture of the work appears, on visual inspection, to be predominantly full ensemble with few timbral changes of importance. It appears that the violins are used to carry the melodic structure and that the woodwinds are primarily harmonic in nature.

Finally, the conductor should consider the fact that the work is a Classical era symphony by Mozart and reflect on what style might be appropriate, what musical elements might be most important in the work, and whether or not extensive interpretation is appropriate to the work.

ANALYSIS

The first step of analysis is to determine the form of the work. As stated above, the second movement is in a sonatina form. A sonatina is described by Wallace Berry in *Form in Music* as "movements in which the middle section, if present at all, is of slight scope and importance, and whose general dimensions are more closely bipartite than tripartite . . . the absence of significant development is the earmark of sonatina movement form."[1] This description very closely matches the Andante of this symphony. Section A contains two primary thematic ideas in measures 1–35. The middle section is transitional in nature, bipartite, and is not developmental of the A section. Neither does it contain significant new melodic material. This section consists of measures 36–49. The section A material returns in a nearly exact recapitulation in measures 50–85.

Knowing the form aids the conductor in determining phrase structure, locating climaxes, and finding the keys used in the work. By looking at the first few measures and the final measures of the work, the conductor should realize that the primary key of the work is G major. Again drawing on knowledge from undergraduate theory and history classes, the conductor should be able to predict that the movement will also use the key of D major as a key center for either the second theme, the middle section of the work, or both. It can also be predicted that the entire recapitulation will remain in the key of G major as was the tradition of the time. Upon examination of the score, the conductor finds just that—the two primary keys are G and D major and they appear at predictable points in the form.

The melodic structure of the work can best be described as ascending arpeggiated primary chords and ascending scalar passages derived from the harmonic structures. The melodic material is very light and gracious with no marcato or legato sections. The melodies are a typical Mozartean mix of lightness and simplicity. There are two primary melodies in the movement, but there are also melodic ideas that serve as transition material and codetta themes.

The harmonic structure of the work is standard, traditional harmony for the time, perhaps even more basic than much of Mozart's music at the time. This might be the case because the original intent of the work was to serve as a serenade for a particular occasion. At any rate, the most adventurous harmonic sounds in the movement are fully diminished seventh chords and an occasional secondary dominant.

Example 8-1 shows an analysis flowchart for the second movement of *Symphony No. 35*.

Example 8-1
Flowchart, *Symphony No. 35, mvt. 2,* Wolfgang Amadeus Mozart.

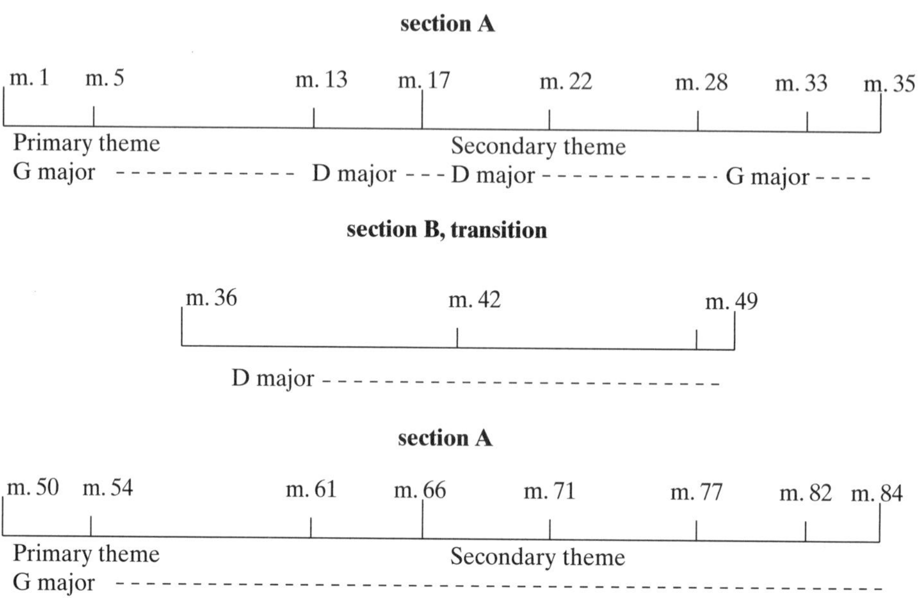

INTERPRETATION

Based upon the analysis and research of the work, the conductor must interpret the work for performance. Each work contains different elements that require interpretive attention. To begin this section of the analysis, the conductor must choose the appropriate tempo for the work. In this movement it appears that only one primary tempo should be used throughout the movement. Mozart made no tempo indications other than "Andante." This instruction, combined with the tradition of playing this type of movement in four beats per bar rather than in two as might be indicated by the meter, leads us to a tempo range of approximately 60–68 beats per minute, with the eighth note receiving one beat. Such a tempo maintains the gracious and light quality of the melody and still provides a "walking tempo" pulse.

Mozart wrote repeat signs at the ends of the two major sections of the work. This was a traditional marking of the day, especially in serenades. However, current practice is to not repeat either of the sections. It should be noted that scholars disagree on this topic, and each conductor must make this decision based upon the best research that he can acquire.

There are several ornaments in the movement that demand interpretation for the performers. These include only two types of basic ornaments: the grace note and the trill. The first of these appear in m. 5 in violin 1. These grace notes (as well as their counterparts in m. 7, 54, and 56) should be played very fast and before the beat. A similar looking ornament in m. 25 and 74 in violin and viola fits better on the beat and fast because of the dotted rhythm and the wedge articulations that follow the ornament. The grace notes added within the descending lines in m. 13, 15, 62, and 64 should be played in rhythm on the beat creating an uninterrupted thirty-second note descending rhythm.

The trills in the movement should all start on the primary note and trill up within the key and without reattacking the primary note. Each trill should return to the primary note to close the trill.

The movement contains several articulation markings, and at least one might be unfamiliar to some musicians—the so-called wedge. Mozart includes staccato markings, wedge articulations, and what might be called portato articulation—the staccato markings underneath a slur. Generally speaking these markings progress from long to short in duration as portato, staccato, wedge. The wedge articulation is the shortest and has the strongest attack of the three. The portato usually indicates an emphasis on each note but not a separation.[2] It is the proper production of these articulations that gives much of the gracious character to the melodies of the work and, therefore, demands the conductor's strict attention to detail.

The dynamic markings in the score are all subito changes. Of special importance are the sforzando/piano markings, such as those in m. 5 and 7. These markings lend emphasis to a particular pulse and/or chord and should be performed as stress accents. This requires that wind players especially produce the stress without a hard tongued accent. The lack of gradual dynamic change markings should not lead the conductor to believe that no crescendi or diminuendi are appropriate in the work. During this time period composers were much less specific with markings, especially dynamics, and relied upon conductors (often the composers themselves) and performers to provide these natural ebb and flow of dynamics as the phrase changed. The conductor should allow the performers this expressive freedom of aiming toward climaxes of phrases and natural tension/release points with dynamics. Once the conductor has discovered the phrase structure of the work, these natural gradual dynamic changes should be added.

The phrase structure of classical music is often thought of as regular and predictable. However, one of the interesting things about Mozart's writing is that his phrases are often of unusual length, while they still sound rounded and regular. This work is an example of this type of irregular, yet regular-sounding phrase structure. The phrases of the formal sections are outlined in Example 8-1. The primary melody of the A section of the movement is sixteen measures long. However, within this regular phrase length the smaller phrases are irregular lengths: four measures, seven measures, and five measures. The secondary melody of the A section is also sixteen measures long. Again, the inner phrases are irregular: five measures, six measures, and five measures. The A section ends with a three-measure concluding theme. The phrases of the secondary section also overlap in that one phrase begins just as the previous phrase cadences.

The short B section of the sonatina serves as transitional material. It is not developmental in nature and also does not have enough thematic material in it to constitute a third theme. This section also sounds regular and is in two seven-measure phrases (or two six-measure overlapping phrases with a two-measure transition to the recapitulation at the end).

The second A section of the work is not a literal recapitulation. However, the phrase structure is the same as the original A section.

Given this information, the conductor can proceed to consider the addition of rubato. In the case of this work it is most appropriate to add slight ritards in tempo as one section transitions into the next. For example, a slight ritard in measures 33 and 34 is appropriate to bring the first A section to a gentle close. The same is true in measures 83 and 84 for the same musical reason. The only other place in the movement where the form indicates a change in pulse is the preparation for the recapitulation in measures 48 and 49.

The conductor might also logically add some change in speed at the climactic spots in the work. Upon analysis of the form, phrase structure, and the following linear analysis, it appears that the climaxes of the work occur in measures 31 and 80. Very minimal pull back in tempo in measures 30 and 79 will help bring out these climaxes. These two points are also examples of where natural crescendi of the lines will aid the climax.

The general rhythm and pulse of the work is stately, reserved, and steady. Much of the rhythmic material is written to create this character. For example, the second violin part of m. 1–10 and the first violin and cello/bass parts of m. 18–21 create steady forward motion. As noted above, few changes in speed are appropriate in this style of work.

The timbre of this work is typical of the works of the period. Winds in pairs was standard orchestral instrumentation of the day. Mozart apparently did not have this number of winds available to him for the original serenade at the Salzburg performance. Perhaps this is why the winds are not really used other than for harmonic purposes. At any rate, it is clear that timbre is not one of the more important musical elements in this work and needs little interpretation.

A linear analysis of the melodies of a work is a good tool for finding the phrase structure and climaxes. The linear analyses in Example 8-2 of the first few measures of both the primary and secondary themes show the important notes of the phrases. This system is based upon the book by Gerald Warfield, *Layer Analysis*.[3] The conductor should ensure that the phrase structure and climaxes he arrives at are supported by the linear analysis.

The "compositional glue" of this work is certainly the melodic structure. As in most works by Mozart, melody is the more important musical element in the sonatina. This fact should guide the conductor to focus more attention on the proper tempo, phrasing, and shading of the melodies of the work.

Example 8-2 Linear analysis, *Symphony No. 35, mvt. 2*, Wolfgang Amadeus Mozart.

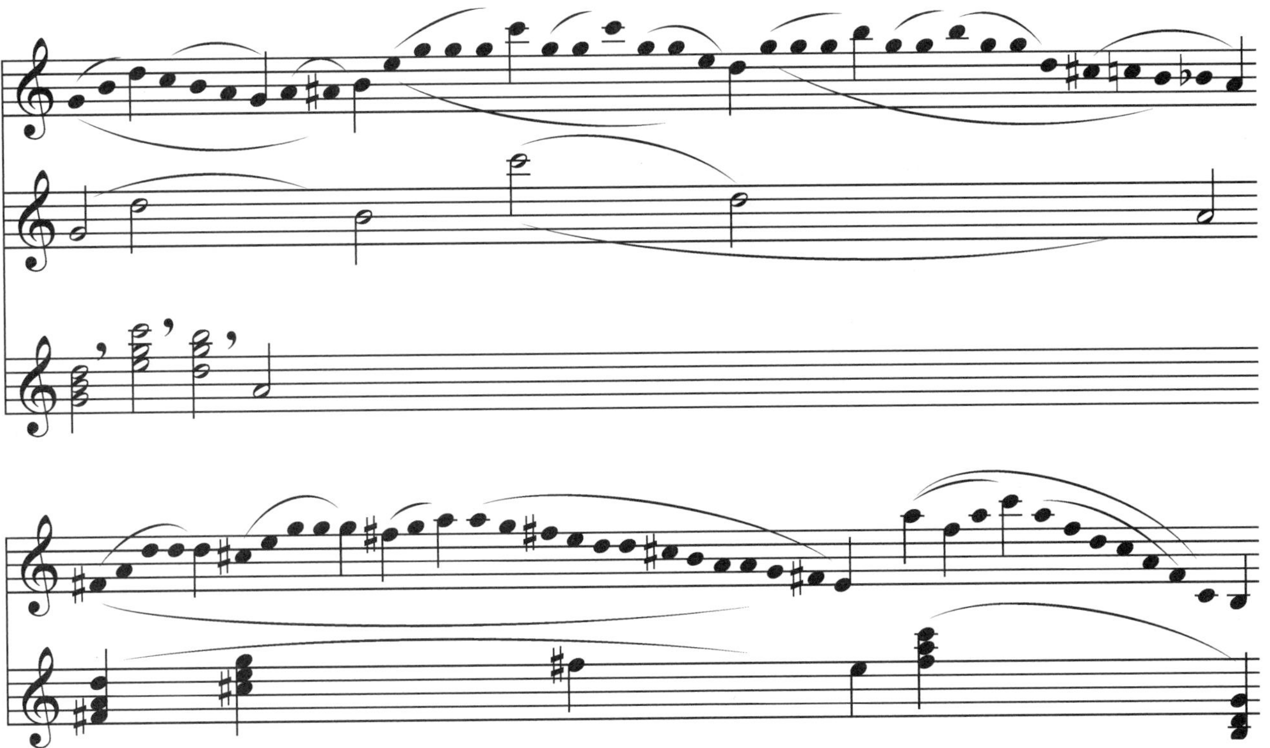

CONDUCTING CHALLENGES

Once the conductor has gained an historical and analytical knowledge of the work, he must identify conducting challenges that occur in the work. In the case of the sonatina, actual physical challenges are few; there are no fermata to deal with, no meter changes, and very few and limited scope tempi changes. The primary challenges of conducting the movement lie in physically matching the gracious and light style of the music—creating gestures that elicit this style from the players. Control of a light and small beat pattern making use of the wrist as a primary hinge will be important.

FIRST SUITE IN E-FLAT FOR MILITARY BAND, CHACONNE, GUSTAV HOLST

OVERVIEW

Gustav Holst wrote several works for wind band, three of which are considered masterworks for the medium: the *First Suite in E-flat*, the *Second Suite in F*, and *Hammersmith*. The title page of the *First Suite* as published provides very little information for the conductor. Instead, it poses questions that the conductor must find answers to with research outside the score. However, the title page does provide at least some suggestions that the conductor can research. For example, the word "first" would indicate that Holst wrote more suites, and though this may not matter to this particular analysis, it is interesting to note. "Suite" might indicate to the conductor that this is a multimovement work (usually more than four movements) and that the movements are only loosely bound together, if at all. (As the conductor progresses through the analysis, he will discover that both of these assumptions are false.) "In E-flat" indicates the primary key of the work. "For Military Band" might indicate a particular instrumentation, usually a more limited instrumentation than the one listed on the score. Further investigation will be needed to determine if the instrumentation has been changed from the original and if those changes are important. The score has two publication dates: 1921 and 1948. Often the first copyright date gives a clue to the actual year in which the work was written, but again, in the case of the *First Suite* this is misleading. Finally, the only other item of interest on the title page is the title of movement one: "Chaconne." At last, a good clue that will assist with the analysis of the work.

A chaconne is usually a set of continuous variations based upon a ground bass in triple meter. The conductor using this description will discover that the work is, in fact, a set of fifteen continuous variations.

In order to find accurate answers to the many questions posed by the title page of the score, the conductor will need to conduct a good deal of external research on this score. Happily, much has been written about this work and its importance to the wind band repertory. The history of the work is shady. Despite the copyright date it is clear that the suite was written in 1909 since Holst himself listed it as Opus 28, no. 1 in his "List of Compositions." But it is unclear why he wrote the work, or who first performed it. One possibility is that Holst wrote it to submit to the Worshipful Company of Musicians, which held a composition contest in 1909 "for military band compositions moulded in the higher forms."[4] If he did, it didn't win an award! It is also possible that it was first performed in 1917 by James Causley Windram, conductor of the 5th Royal Northumberland Fusiliers. The *Second Suite in F* is dedicated to Windram, and he was instrumental in getting the *First Suite* published. Letters from Holst mention Windram and question whether or not he needs a score to the suite.[5] According to his biographer and daughter Imogen Holst, the work may have been first heard and composed for the Festival at the People's Palace, Mile End, London, in May 1909. Or, the work may have just been a response to the call for quality new works for military band made by the bandmaster of Kneller Hall, the Royal Military School of Music. But no record of the actual first performance or reason for composition exists. The first record of a concert performance is on June 23, 1920, at Kneller Hall by the 165-member (!) Royal Military School of Music band. The work was obviously well known and appreciated by this time because in the following year, 1921, it was published by Boosey & Hawkes. In 1948 the work was reinstrumented and republished. This version adds instruments to the then standard symphonic band instrumentation and deletes instruments no longer in use at the time such as the bombardon and baritone horn. This reissuing of the work also deleted several things from the title page. For example, in the original Holst made three notes to conductors, all of which were deleted in the 1948 score. Two concern leaving out certain instruments and are only interesting, but the first note is important: "As each movement is founded on the same phrase it is requested that the Suite be played right through without a break."[6] To the conductor this says that all the movements are connected, unusual in a suite, and that Holst wanted the movements performed without break. A good deal has been written about the words "without a break." Did Holst mean without pause, with a short pause, or was he simply saying that another activity should not be placed in between the movements when performed. This last possibility apparently was common in military bands of the time. Movements of works might be interrupted by parades, ceremonies, or other military proceedings. It is possible that Holst was simply telling military bandmasters that this kind of long break between movements was inappropriate since the work's movements are related thematically.

Holst also wrote "time of performance 11 minutes" in the original score, and this does not appear in the 1948 version. This gives the conductor a general idea of tempi of the three movements, which are simply labeled "Allegro moderato," "Vivace," and "Tempo di Marci," respectively.

ANALYSIS

The chaconne of the *First Suite in E-flat* is a series of continuous variations on the first eight measures. These opening bars are at the same time melodic in nature and serve as a ground bass or ostinato pattern on which the chaconne is built. There are fifteen variations: twelve are strict and are in E-flat major, two are inversions in c minor, and one is based in the dominant. The melody on which the movement is based is legato and haunting. It progresses from tonic to dominant, making it perfect for a continuous variation because it does not end with a cadence.

Variation one, for brass (m. 9–16), is in E-flat major and adds both harmonic structure to the original and an important counterline in cornet. It, like the original, is lyrical, subdued, and soft.

Variation two, for woodwinds (m. 17–24), is also in E-flat. Alhough harmonic structures are created in this variation, it, like much of Holst's work, is linear in nature and polyphonic sounding. In addition to the original, this variation is made up of three other woodwind lines that weave in and out of the original but do not change its style.

Variation three for mixed brass and woodwinds (m. 25–32) is a stylistic variation. Holst adds fanfare-like staccato woodwind and brass material to the lyrical original. This variation is also in E-flat major.

Variation four (m. 33– 40) is scored for full band, including percussion, and continues in E-flat. It continues the overall crescendo begun in variation three that climaxes in variation five. This variation is in the same style as variation three and sounds like a continuation of that variation, with more forces involved.

Variation five (m. 41–48) is the high point of the first half of the movement. Also in E-flat, Holst creates the variation by shortening the length of notes of the original and harmonizing the theme in brass and combining this with woodwind continuous scales.

Variation six (m. 49–56) is still in E-flat and is primarily for brass choir (along with bass clarinet and bassoon doubling the bass line). The variation is again created in two ways: (1) by harmonization of the original and (2) by the addition of a running eighth note bass line. The end of this variation serves as a transition into a return to the more lyrical and brooding character of the original when variation seven begins. (m. 57–64). This thinly scored variation offers up a new counter-melody in clarinet to accompany the horn solo line of the original. The variation is based in E-flat.

Variation eight (m. 65–72) is the final E-flat original prior to the introduction of the inversion variations. The variation of the original is created by a triplet offset counterline duet in flute and oboe. The entire variation (except for two measures of horn 1) is scored in woodwinds.

Variation nine (m. 73–80) is the first of two inversion variations in c minor. This variation is a literal inversion of the original, and it is amazing how lyrical and melodic this inversion sounds—a true melody equal to the original.

Variation ten (m. 81–88) continues the c minor inversion now scored in brass and adds a bass line that feels like it is in two beats per bar, rather than the triple meter of the movement.

Variation eleven (m. 89–96) returns to the original theme, but this time the theme is in the dominant. In so doing Holst creates a variation of the original that follows the shape and basic intervallic structure of the original but has some altered intervals as he stays within the key signature.

Variation twelve (m. 97–104) is the return of the true original theme in E-flat major played over a B-flat pedal. This section begins the build up to the second major climax of the movement in variation fourteen.

Variation thirteen (m. 105–113) is for full ensemble, is in E-flat major, with a continuing dominant pedal. Combined with variation twelve it creates a sixteen-measure crescendo in dynamics and intensity to variation fourteen.

Variation fourteen (m. 114–121) is the climactic section of the second half of the movement. Scored for full ensemble, it contains four lines that serve as counterlines to the original. Holst's linear compositional skill is at its height in these final bars of the movement, creating what seems at the same time to be a harmonic and polyphonic structure above the original theme.

Variation fifteen (m. 122–end) contains the work's largest climax, which continues for seven measures without resolution until the final measure. This statement of the theme with its opening on the dominant and its altered intervals over an E-flat pedal creates the sense of a seven-measure-long dominant chord. Holst varies the fourth and fifth intervals of the theme by adding a flat to the fifth note of the melody. The upward resolution of the tension on the final chord provides a surprisingly brilliant release to end the movement.

As can be seen by this brief formal outline, the primary keys of the movement are E-flat major and c minor.

The melodic structure of the work is the most important musical element. Not only are all the variations of this movement based upon the chaconne theme, but the melodies of movements two and three are also derived from these same intervals. Holst's skill as a composer of linear music is evident in this movement. There is actually very little harmonic material. Instead, the harmonies that exist are often created by the polyphonic settings of the original with counterlines. There appear to be no unusual harmonic structures in the work.

Example 8-3 Flowchart, *First Suite in E-flat, Chaconne,* Gustav Holst.

m. 1	m. 9	m. 17	m. 25	m. 33	m. 41	m. 49	m. 57	m. 65	m. 72
Theme	v.1	v.2	v.3	v.4	v.5	v.6	v.7	v.8	
E-flat									
Low brass	brass	w. wind	fanfares	full ens.	Short, chordal	homophonic	lyrical	triplet	
p	p	pp	mf	FF	FF	FF	p	p	

m. 73	m. 81	m. 89	m. 97	m. 105	m. 114	m. 122
Theme	v.10	v.11	v.12	v.13	v.14	v.15
c-minor		dominant	E-flat			theme on V w/D flat
inversion	inversion	altered interval	original	full ensemble to end		
p	p	p	p	cresc.	FF	FF

The rhythmic structure of the work is one of continuous forward motion. This feeling is created by the melodic structure of the work. Since the chaconne theme ends on the dominant and is always followed by another chaconne variation, there is no stopping this forward-moving rhythmic pulse. The lyrical and fluid nature of the chaconne theme contributes to this feeling as well.

Timbre appears to be an important aspect of this work. In fact, it is used as a technique of variation. Holst sometimes contrasts whole variations of one wind choir against an opposite wind choir in the next variation. In general, the timbre of this work is a dark quality befitting the somber nature of the chaconne theme. This makes the final chord, with its upward resolution, even more brilliant in contrast and serves as an excellent bridge to the bright quality of the second movement.

Clearly, the compositional glue of this movement, in fact the entire piece, is the intervallic structure of the chaconne theme.

Example 8-4 Linear analysis, *First Suite in E-flat for Military Band, Chaconne,* Gustav Holst.

INTERPRETATION

The tempo indication provided by Holst for the Chaconne is "Allegro moderato." In order to interpret this marking, the conductor should consider the style of each of the variations and set one tempo that works for each of them. There is only one other tempo indication in the score, "rit. al Fine," first at variation fourteen and again at variation 15 (unless one considers the term "Maestoso" to be a tempo rather than a style marking at variation fourteen). The tempo chosen should allow the theme to flow steadily forward without feeling lugubrious. Too slow a tempo will tend to segregate each of the eight-measure variation phrases and create a work that sounds "chopped up" rather than flowing forward. The tempo of quarter note equals 88 beats per minute works well to achieve this goal.

Holst only suggests rubato near the end of the work with the marking "rit al Fine," as identified in the previous paragraph. Like choosing a tempo that is too slow, adding much rubato to the work will also cause it to lose its forward and continuous motion. The only added rubato suggested by the analysis might be a small ritard in measures 71–72 to enhance the form. This is the end of the first half of the work and is followed by the two inversion variations.

The work's phrase structure is very clearly eight-measure phrases divided into two four-measure subphrases. Each of the variations has this same structure although the last three variations are nine measures in length, a device that increases the tension that builds to the end of the work and to the second of only two real cadences. (The other is at the end of variation eight immediately preceding the inversion variations.)

Holst uses instrumentation and dynamics to lead the work to its major climaxes. The first occurs at variation 5 with the full ensemble playing at the highest dynamic level of the work so far. This climax is the height of a four-variation build-up in dynamics, instrumentation, and intensity that is followed by a three-variation reverse of this process. This causes the theme and variations one through eight to create a sort-of arch that builds to the climax in variation five and relaxes to the end of variation eight—halfway through the work.

The second major climax of the work occurs at variation fourteen and follows a five-variation build much like that in the first half of the work. This time, rather than following this build with a relaxation, Holst continues to increase the intensity and creates the largest and most important climax of the work in variation fifteen. The intensity created by full ensemble, double forte dynamic, and the statement of the theme starting on the fifth rather than the tonic drives this climax all the way to the final measure. The resolution of the climax upward rather than a relaxation down (as might be more normal) is startling, yet brilliant. It also matches perfectly with Holst's request to perform the movements without break because the resolution of movement 1 actually acts as a preparation chord for movement 2. The proper control of these multivariation crescendi and builds in intensity will be the primary interpretive and conducting challenge for the conductor.

This work contains no ornaments, and the articulations are plainly marked and are standard for the time period. The theme appears in slurred, short, and legato versions in the work. Holst is very economical with use of articulations. Only two accent marks appear in the entire movement (m. 127 and 128).

One of the major areas of interpretive concern for the conductor is the balancing of lines within the variations. Holst was, more than anything else, a linear composer. This movement is indicative of this style, and several of the variations require close attention to balance in order to hear the interweaving of these lines with the theme. This begins as early as the first and second variations. In variation one the cornets present two independent lines on top of the theme. The same happens in variation two in woodwinds with three independent lines. Each variation's complexity and beauty is created by these interweaving lines.

The Chaconne contains a few isolated motifs that may need the conductor's attention in order to be heard. The cornet and trombone solo fanfares in variation three are often covered by the woodwind section if not brought out. The same is true of the ascending trombone line in measures 31–32 that end variation three.

CONDUCTING CHALLENGES

Conducting challenges in the work are more interpretive in nature than physical. However, the conductor must be able to produce a very economically sized and lyrical 3/4 pattern for several of the variations, and at the same time change to indicate a crisp staccato or heavy pesante style. These style changes are the most physically demanding aspect of the work. And, several of the variations (e.g., three, four, five, and six) mix two contrasting musical styles.

The other general physical conducting challenge might be the number of cues that are necessary. The variety of styles and timings of cues is difficult. The conductor must be able to cue entrances on any beat and for syncopated entrances in at least four different styles: lyrical, staccato, pesante, and maestoso. The Chaconne is an excellent training work for conductors because it requires the conductor to create tension across long time periods while still attending to short-term issues.

NOTES

1. Berry, Wallace. *Form in Music*, Prentice Hall, Englewood Cliffs, NJ, 1966, pp. 231–232.
2. Brown, Clive. *Classical and Romantic Performance Practice 1750–1900*. Oxford University Press, New York, 1999.
3. Warfield, Gerald. *Layer Analysis: a Primer of Elementary Tonal Structures*, Longman, New York, 1976.
4. Mitchell, Jon C. *From Kneller Hall to Hammersmith. The Band Works of Gustav Holst.* Hans Schneider, Tutzing, 1990.
5. Ibid.
6. Ibid.

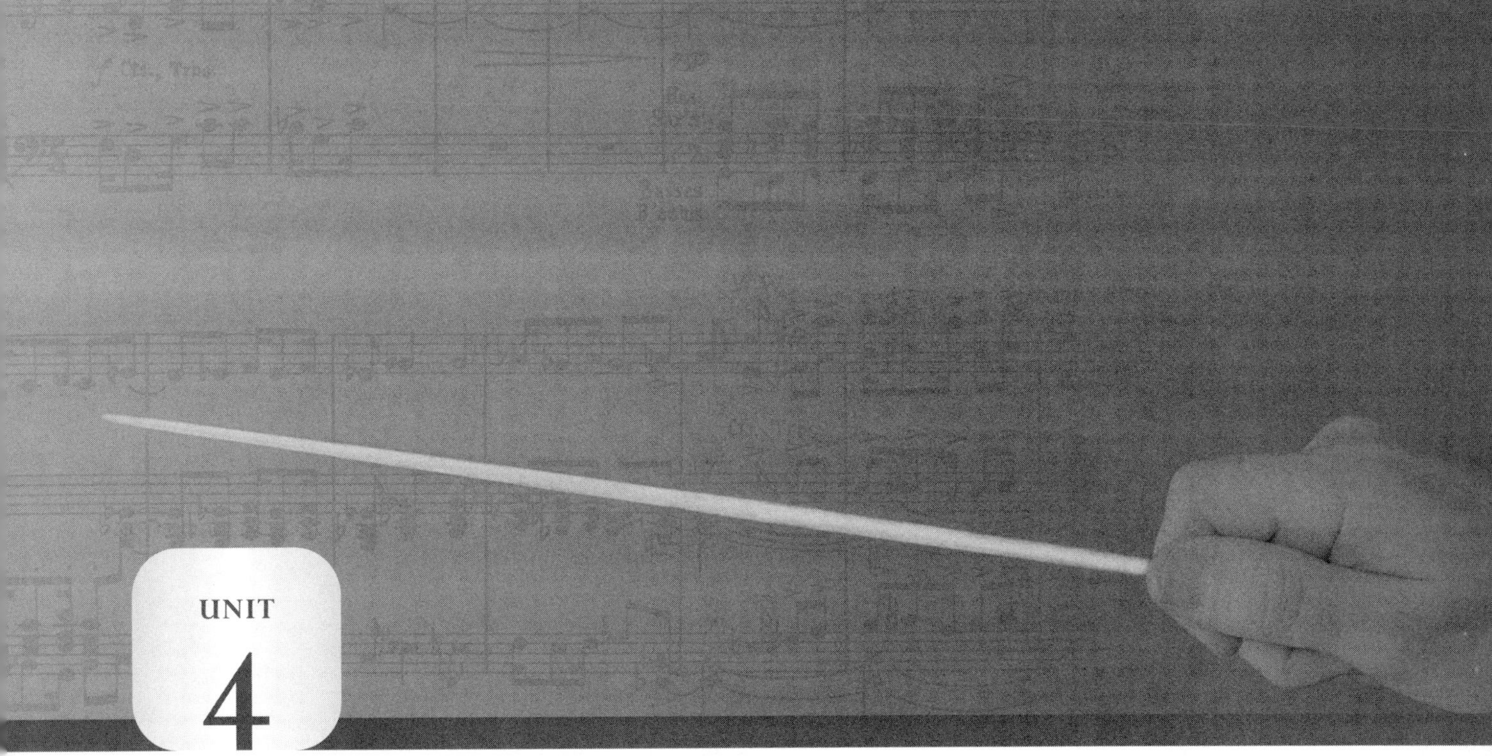

UNIT 4

Error Detection *and* Correction

CHAPTER 9

Aural Skills and Error Detection

Perhaps the most important task of the conductor is the detection and correction of errors. The ability to successfully perform this task is based upon three things: score preparation, knowledge of performer and instrument error tendencies, and the ability to easily move from a focused listening to a more generic listening.

Music schools provide training in both aural skills and conducting, but despite the obvious connection, integration of these skills rarely happens in music classes. When asked to conduct a live group for the first time, many students are unprepared to apply any aural skills learned in ear-training courses and are often confused by the total sound of the ensemble. The task of mastering the technique of conducting, leading an ensemble, inspiring a large group of people, and detecting and correcting a wide variety of errors is a difficult one, but one that becomes easier with experience.

The new conductor might notice that it seems to be easier to hear errors when not on the podium in front of the ensemble, or when not looking at a score. This is an indication that conducting technique is not yet mastered and/or score preparation is not adequate.

In general, conductors focus their aural energies on five error types: note and rhythm errors, intonation problems, and errors of balance and articulation. Often they tend to these errors in that order. Unfortunately, this is the reverse of the order of frequency of errors produced in most ensembles. Articulation and balance errors are the most common ensemble errors and the least often corrected. Each of these error types is studied separately in the exercises in Chapter 10.

RHYTHMIC AND TEMPO ERRORS

Errors of this type fall into three general categories: misplayed rhythms, incorrect rests, and errors of tempo. Rhythmic errors most often, but not always, are caused by lack of preparation on the part of the performer or by the complexity of the rhythm itself. Both can be fixed by the performer taking the time to analyze the rhythm. However, in an ensemble often the performer is "reading" the rhythm rather than playing a rhythm that he has actually prepared. This "reading" is only as good as the rhythmic experience level of the player. This is because performers tend to read a grouping of notes as a rhythmic pattern that they have encountered before (whether or not it is) based on the appearance of the rhythm.

Another common type of error is pattern reversal. For example, performers commonly reverse the pattern shown in Example 9-1a and play the more commonly seen pattern shown in Example 9-1b.

Example 9.1
(a) and (b)

Most often pattern reversal occurs when the appearance of a series of notes resembles a more commonly used rhythm and is embedded within a larger rhythmic structure.

Pattern continuation is also an oft-heard error. This occurs when a rhythmic pattern resembles in appearance an already established pattern. The performer fails to recognize that the pattern has changed and continues playing the older pattern. The passage in Example 9.2 might create such an error in measure 2 where the pattern becomes reversed. Errors of this type are difficult to detect because they do not create "ensemble chaos." The rhythms look and sound similar, and the error actually creates a mistake that is much more difficult to detect: an accent error.

Example 9.2

Performers are often confused when the speed of the appearance of the rhythm does not match the actual performance speed. This can be illustrated by Claude Debussy's *Prelude to the Afternoon of a Faun* (Example 9-3). To the musician unfamiliar with this melody the line appears to move much faster than it should in actual performance, due mainly to the complexity of the notation.

Example 9.3 *Prelude to the Afternoon of a Faun,* Claude Debussy.

Rhythmic errors also often occur when the speed of the pulse seems to not match the meter of the work. This happens frequently when, for example, a passage in 2/4 is actually played in four. The performer tends to not make the pulse change required and plays twice as fast as is appropriate. This is a tendency of many performers—to play length of pitches the same regardless of meter and pulse. For example, inexperienced players tend to play an eighth note the same length in both 6/8 and 2/4 time because they do not understand that the meter actually changes the note value.

Notes that are tied together seem to cause many rhythmic errors. These often create complex syncopations that the performer needs to work out slowly and individually. Or the performer simply needs to count while playing—often performers see a tied note and make a general guess at its length rather than actually maintaining the real pulse in their heads while playing the rhythm.

Errors caused by the presence of rests are also common. Most often this type of error is an "entrance error," one where the performer is either early (most common) or late in entering after a series of long rests. Many entrance errors are made by groups of players rather than individuals. If the conductor is relying on one of the musicians in the ensemble to provide the "correct version" of the rhythm rather than an internal version of their own, he will tend to not detect entrance errors.

Another type of rest-related error is when the rest is embedded in the rhythm itself.

Example 9.4

Performers should be encouraged to view the rests as simply silent notes and to "play" the rests. This incorporates the rest into the rhythmic structure.

Errors of tempo are either rushing or dragging errors. Both are common, and both are directly related to the technique of the player and the complexity of the rhythmic line.

Often the cause of tempo errors is the conductor. Inexperienced conductors often follow rather than lead the ensemble. In large ensembles this allows the pulse to change at the will of a constantly changing group of players and is often affected by their technical skill, or lack thereof. This usually results in a slowing of tempo. Ensembles, when left to themselves, often gravitate to one of three rather standard and comfortable tempi: quarter note equals 72, 120, or 144.

Many performers seem to think that the smaller the note, the faster it should be played, regardless of context. This, of course, causes many errors in tempo, most often rushing.

Performers, in general, seem to share tendencies where error production is concerned. For example, they tend to "follow the leader." Weaker players tend to make the same errors that section leaders do, and once a rhythmic error has begun it is often continued in other sections or parts.

Long pitches are often rushed, and long note value pitches are often released too early.

Descending lines tend to accelerate and unison lines tend to rush.

Late entrances are common in music that is imitative. For example, subject entrances within a fugue often are played late, and quite often the tempo of the new entry is slower than that of the existing line.

Dotted rhythms tend to be lengthened in duration, most commonly overlengthening the dotted note. Quite often the performer actually doubles the note value.

Rhythms in compound meter are often played as if they are notated in simple meter.

Performers also tend to make adjustments to make up for their errors. If a note is held too long, the player might skip the next few notes or rush the next line in order to make the entire passage end at the correct moment. They also tend to "cover" for other players, adjusting their tempo and line to match with something that another player has altered. Frequently performers execute rhythms inaccurately because they are trying to match rhythms with another ensemble member whose rhythm they believe to be the same as their own. This error often occurs in the performance of dotted or syncopated rhythm patterns. Because the error actually creates rhythmic "harmony" in the ensemble, it is difficult to hear. Performers that create chaos are easier to correct than those that manage to make their rhythms work out over time or match them with other players' parts.

Likewise, conductors share some error tendencies. Conductors tend to hear an early entrance easier than a late entrance because an early entrance intrudes on an already established pattern.

Rhythmic errors in music of a homophonic nature tend to be easier to detect than errors in polyphonic music. This is less a problem of visual recognition for the conductor than one of conception of the composite rhythm created by individual lines. Many conductors are successful in detecting errors in single-line rhythms but fail to hear the composite rhythm. This problem probably relates to the fact that few musicians ever see more than one line at a time in their own performance experience. Only in the theory classroom, class piano, and conducting are students asked to read a score, and then probably without any instruction in how to do so.

In contrast, some rhythmic errors are difficult to hear because the performer accents the line correctly or adjusts the lengths of other pitches in order for the line to end at the correct time but performs some rhythms within the line inaccurately. This is a much more complex problem for the conductor to hear because the performer has combined accurate performance with aspects of incorrect execution.

Many rhythmic errors go undetected because of a more basic problem—the balance of the ensemble is so bad that the conductor cannot hear anything clearly. This is a problem for the players also, who often can correct their own errors if the conductor can balance the ensemble so that the players can hear themselves.

Many conductors find it easier to hear errors of rushing a tempo than dragging a tempo. This may be due to the fact that conductors must hear ahead of the ensemble and when a group catches up with the hearing of the conductor, he notices it better than when a group gets further behind the beat pattern.

Errors that don't create chaos are hard to detect. Many errors in rhythm are either played too softly to hear or they do not disrupt the rhythmic flow or pulse of the work.

Conductors create some performer errors with their technique. Poor technique usually causes slowing in tempo but can also create certain beats within a pattern to be hurried or slowed.

To improve error detection of rhythmic problems, the conductor must combine preparation with ease on the podium and experience. Even the most basic of errors are difficult to detect if the conductor does not have a definite sound in his head of what the work should sound like.

The improvement of conducting technique will also solve many rhythmic errors, especially those of rushing, dragging, and early/late entrances from rests.

The conductor must learn to read multiple layers of rhythms as a composite rhythm and hear that rhythmic structure while conducting. This might best be achieved by practicing singing one rhythmic line while clapping another. This allows the conductor to create a composite rhythm but still hear one as primary and one as secondary in nature.

Visualize rests as silent notes, not stopping or resting points.

Use this information to predict errors through score study. Study places in the score that are rhythmically complex or that might cause players to fall into one of the traps mentioned above. Then, while conducting, shift your aural focus to rhythm and briefly ignore other musical elements in order to detect what the players are doing.

Fix balance first. Many rhythmic errors will be fixed by the players if only they can hear themselves and how their parts fit into the overall rhythmic structure.

PITCH ERRORS

All performers focus most of their energies on producing the right notes. Likewise, novice conductors spend a good deal of their time and energy listening for and correcting note errors, sometimes to the exclusion of correcting errors of intonation, balance, dynamics, and intonation. Yet, of the five primary error types, note errors occur with the least frequency.

There are at least five different categories of pitch errors (not including intonation within the term "pitch"). First and most common are simply incidental wrong notes. These happen in every rehearsal and most performances for a variety of reasons: a player loses concentration and depresses the wrong key, the player has an instrument or embouchure problem, the player misreads a line, etc. These errors are the easiest to detect because they stick out. Usually they do not require the conductor to stop and point them out to the performer. In fact, often to do so is simply wasting time. They are also the most frustrating to conductors because they are random, individual errors that can't be predicted and for which there is no real "fix."

Also extremely common are errors in pitch caused by missed key signatures and/or accidentals. Also usually glaringly obvious, these errors usually are worth stopping for, if for no other reason than to allow the player to mark the music with some reminder. Unfortunately, these errors, like random pitch errors, also never end despite the quality of the ensemble.

So-called partial errors are most common on brass instruments but are also possible on string instruments. On a brass instrument this refers to the player playing on a different partial of the overtone series than is indicated in the music. The player has the correct fingering or position but the embouchure is not producing the correct note. These errors are sometimes very hard to detect, especially for the player, because they rarely cause chaos. The wrong note often is an acceptable note in the chord and will only sound out of place when heard in a linear context.

Note errors are also caused by the limitations in range of certain players. Sometimes the part goes outside the comfortable range of a player, causing the player to miss the note, usually very obviously.

An error in chord quality is often produced by one of the above-mentioned errors. A player who misses a key signature or plays the wrong partial can sometimes change the quality of chord, most often between major and minor.

Like the production of rhythmic errors, performers also have some common tendencies where pitch errors are concerned. All performers tend to occasionally miss key signatures and accidentals. Most brass players make partial errors—the over- or undershooting of a correct note. Performers regularly misread a scalar line that changes scales within the line. And many performers make note errors because they read the contour of a melodic line rather than the specific notes of the line.

Conductors also share common problems of pitch error detection. Many conductors find it easier to hear individual note errors than group or section errors. This problem indicates that the conductor does not have a strong enough internal concept of the melody and is relying on some performer to recreate a correct version for him. In this case, if an entire section makes the error, it will usually go undetected.

Not all intervals are used equally in music. Some are used much more frequently than others, and we tend to hear those better. Many conductors find it easier to detect errors involving thirds, fifths, and unisons than they do tritones, sixths, and sevenths.

Conductors are also better at reading the general melodic curve than hearing the specific intervals of the line. This problem causes the general acceptance of any large sounding leap to be heard as correct for intervals of the sixth, seventh, or larger.

Conductors tend to listen to outer voices more than inner sounds. This is probably because, for the most part, the harmonic language is set by the bass line and the melody is often in the highest part. Hearing errors in inner lines takes focused listening.

Conductors tend to hear errors more easily when played by instruments in the range of their own instrument.

Individual errors are easier to hear than group errors because an individual error creates some kind of "clash" and stands out.

Conductors hear errors that create linear problems better than they do errors that create vertical reconstruction. And they hear errors more easily in lines that they perceive as being of a melodic nature.

Conductors tend to hear more pitch errors when the music is played at a slower tempo than in a fast passage.

Improving detection of pitch errors is usually a matter of better score preparation and focused listening. Perhaps most important, the conductor should fix problems of balance and intonation so that the performers can hear the pitch errors themselves. Other than partial errors, most pitch errors will be corrected by the players themselves, if they can hear them.

Improving interval discrimination will assist the conductor in hearing pitch errors. An excellent method of learning intervals is to sing major and minor scales, maintaining a fundamental pitch that is returned to between each scale tone. It is important to note that singing, rather than playing, is suggested. An instrument will mechanically produce a reasonably accurate interval without the aid of the ears. In order to sing an interval the musician must first be able to hear it. Or try singing an interval followed by its inversion and singing chords arpeggiated in each inversion.

Conductors often have difficulty hearing errors in the harmonic structure because these errors are obscured by other problems. For example, the doubling of parts in most ensembles creates a thick, full sound that tends to hide errors. Note errors in a harmonic structure might also be obscured by poor intonation. Intonation problems often mask errors that have created chord quality changes. Working on intonation improvement exercises each day will actually help improve the detection of note errors.

Visually relating the outline of a melody to chords can also improve a conductor's harmonic hearing. Often the important pitches of a melody outline a chord or harmonic progression. Reading melodies in this manner helps provide the conductor with an expected sound with which to compare the actual sounds produced.

INTONATION ERRORS

When asked to name the most frustrating problem within their ensemble, most conductors answer "intonation." This frustration is usually not based on the performers' lack of good intonation but on the conductor's inability to correct intonation problems. Many conductors are able to hear when intonation problems exist, but fewer have the ability to instruct the performers on how to correct the problems.

Intonation problems are often closely linked to problems of balance and blend. The conductor should correct these errors before any other types in order to give the performers an opportunity to hear the problems of the ensemble.

When it comes to hearing and correcting intonation problems, conductor and performer tendencies are the same. Most musicians tend to hear flat sounds more easily than sharp sounds. This problem often causes ensembles to play above the standard A = 440 pitch. It also causes many conductors to accept sharp sounds as correct because most players spend their lives playing sharp.

Conductors and performers usually perceive the higher note of an interval as being correct in terms of intonation. Probably because musicians are trained to tune to a "high" instrument (i.e., clarinet or oboe), this often creates a very bright sound in an ensemble and tends to push the pitch higher. Tuning the octave is an excellent example of a higher pitch naturally dominating a lower one. This happens because the lower pitch has more low overtones in it. This can be changed with dynamics.

The softer a pitch is played, the fewer high overtones are audible. This is why when trying to balance an octave the upper player has to play softer than the lower player.

The natural dynamics of intervals are also important to achieve good intonation. When two pitches are played together, one will always dominate the other. This is caused by the presence of combination tones. Combination tones are present in all intervals, but are most often heard in the major sixth and minor sixth. These tones are produced from the combination of the frequencies of the two pitches being played. For example, in a perfect fifth the combination tone produced is an octave below the lowest note of the interval, causing the bottom note of the perfect fifth to dominate. The opposite is true of the perfect fourth.

Hearing intonation of closed intervals is easier for most musicians than open intervals. Because of the registers in bands and orchestras, conductors must learn to hear open intervals as well.

Some intervals are easier to tune than others. This is due to the number of overtones that the notes of an interval share: the more common overtones there are, the easier the interval is to tune. For example, the overtones of the octave and unison match, the notes of a P5 share four overtones, the pitches of a P4 share three, and notes making up a M3, m3, M6, and M2 share two overtones. The m6 and m7 pitches have one overtone in common, and the m2, M7, and tritone share none. This means that the unison should be easier to tune than the P4, and the P4 is easier than the tritone to play in tune. When teaching intonation the conductor should begin with intervals that have the most shared overtones. Once performers are successful with the octave, unison, P5, and P4 they can move on to the more complex intervals.

Instrumentalists tend to hear intonation of similar timbres better than dissimilar timbres. This is because an instrument's timbre is largely made up of the overtones present. It follows that two instruments whose overtones match are easier to tune than those that have few overtones in common. This is why it is easier for two flute players to play in tune together than one flute and one tuba.

Most musicians are trained to tune vertically, that is, to try to play their pitch in tune in a chord or other vertical structure. But few ever spend much time trying to play a horizontal line in tune. Musical training is more focused on playing in tune with another player than it is on a performer playing a melodic line in tune. Most conductors are much more successful at tuning two or more simultaneous pitches than they are in tuning two successive pitches.

Most causes of poor intonation can be traced to training. Ear-training courses in colleges provide no instruction in this important aural skill. Some performers learn tendencies of their own instruments in studio lessons. Almost all musicians have the ability to hear when they are out of tune. What they lack is the ability to tell which direction to move to correct the problem.

Often intonation problems are caused by an inability to "read" the intervals. A large interval such as a M7 is just viewed as a large leap without any real idea on the performer's part of what that interval sounds like before executing it. Generally, a descending wide leap is expanded producing a flat low tone. When making an ascending large leap players often compress the interval, resulting in the high note being flat.

Performers often allow the pitch of an ascending line to get sharper as the line gets higher and allow descending lines to go flatter as the notes descend.

As has been stated earlier, lack of good balance and blend create error-detection problems. Usually, an ensemble will play more in tune once the balance has been corrected. This happens for several reasons, but the primary one is probably that the performers have a much more focused and blended sound to try to fit their sound into once the ensemble is balanced.

One of the most successful methods of improving intonation is to become familiar with intonation tendencies of the instruments in the ensemble. The performers must become familiar with the specific tendencies of their individual instruments. This allows the conductor to anticipate problems and to be able to assist the players by suggesting typical solutions to problems. For example, written D5 is flat on all B-flat trumpets. The player should attempt to raise this pitch in order to play it exactly in tune. However, if the player is playing this D as part of a B-flat chord, he should probably not raise the pitch because, as the D is the third of the chord, it should be played a bit flat in order for the chord to sound in tune.

Tuning to a low pitch within the ensemble makes it easier, long term, for players to tune chords and other lines. This also helps the ensemble's overall pitch to keep from rising and enables the ensemble to achieve a darker tone quality.

Intervals and pitches must be adjusted according to their function in the key structure and chord structure. For example, a performer sustaining an F throughout the chord progression F, g7, d, B-flat, F cannot keep the F at a constant pitch or the chords will be out of tune. Performers often are faced with the choice of sacrificing a linear intonation in order to be in tune with a vertical structure. Conductors should learn the adjustments required for intervals to sound in tune. For example, the interval of a M3 should be contracted in a major chord in order for the chord to sound in tune. Example 9.5 indicates adjustments that should be made to intervals in chords.

In rehearsals the conductor can improve intonation by performing lines without rhythm or articulation. Focusing all aural energies on timbre, balance, and intonation is a very successful exercise for most ensembles.

Example 9.5 Interval Adjustment Chart.

Interval	Number of common overtones	Adjustment required to be in tune
m2	None	
M2	None	
m3	Two	Interval should be expanded
M3	Two	Interval should be contracted
P4	Three	Interval should be contracted
Tritone	None	Most players should expand this interval
P5	Four	Interval should be expanded
m6	One	Interval should be expanded
M6	One	Interval should be contracted
m7	One	Most players should contract this interval
M7	None	Interval should be expanded
Octave	All	No adjustment necessary

Tuning instruments in groups of like timbre and range usually assists less inexperienced players. Tuning the brass section first by instrument, then by choir, and finally adding them to the full ensemble will help players play in tune. Again, this is due to the fact that the more common overtones that exist in a sound the easier the sound is to tune.

Most musicians are familiar with the "beat principle" of tuning. Two players can hear audible pulsations when playing an interval out of tune. The slower they can make the pulsations, the closer in tune they are. This is much more effective between two like instruments than with different timbres.

Each of these methods of improving intonation is time-consuming, but the results will be significant and the performers will be more able to correct their own errors, allowing the conductor to focus more energy on interpreting the music.

DYNAMIC ERRORS

Among the most common and least detected/corrected types of errors are errors in dynamics. The number of these errors is rivaled only by articulation errors. Errors of dynamics are often not corrected at all and rarely on a consistent basis.

Errors in dynamics cause other errors, especially problems with balance and blend of the ensemble. They also often cause intonation errors both for the player making the dynamic error and for other performers, who then mistakenly tune their pitches to that first player.

Most dynamic errors are simply the omission of dynamic change. A great many players play all passages between the ranges of mezzo piano and mezzo forte without really making use of other dynamic ranges. The conductor will need to do a good deal of consistent coaxing to get most ensembles to play a true piano or forte dynamic. This lack of perceptible change in volume creates another error—lack of expression.

When performers do make errors of dynamics that are outside the printed range, they are usually too loud. It is a very rare player that inherently plays a line softer than indicated or required. This is very common in the extreme ranges of most wind instruments.

Generally speaking, the higher the part, the louder it will be played and vice versa. Performers tend to crescendo as their lines ascend and decrescendo when they descend. (Many times this is an appropriate expression, but this "roller coaster" style of dynamics cannot become the norm for the ensemble.)

Performers also tend to "follow the leader" in their performance of dynamics. If they hear other lines getting louder or softer, they often follow along regardless of what is indicated in their own part. In some instances this can be used to the conductor's advantage, especially in his attempt to achieve a balanced and blended sound if the "leader" happens to be a cellist or tubaist.

Conductors also have common tendencies in how they detect and correct dynamic errors. As with the detection of most errors, many conductors hear these errors in outer lines more easily than inner parts. Because these lines tend to carry the bass line and the melody, they get more of our attention. But this tendency to place our focus here also creates ensembles that lack a balanced middle and sometimes have an upper-dominated tone quality.

Conductors more often detect and correct sounds that are too loud than those that are too soft. This problem generates from the desire of the conductor to change any sound that intrudes on his mental concept of the music. Unless the soft sound causes such an interruption to the recording playing in the conductor's head, the sound that is too soft often goes uncorrected. Related to this problem, conductors often hear dynamic changes that are not actually taking place. Because conductors are looking at a score and are expecting dynamic changes, they often think they are hearing them when they really aren't. Or they often accept very minimal changes in dynamics as acceptable. This creates, over time, a very limited dynamic range from the ensemble—one where the group never plays a real forte or piano. Most changes in dynamics have to be exaggerated in order for the regular listener to detect them.

Errors in terraced dynamics are easier to detect than errors that involve a gradual change in dynamics. This is probably because terraced dynamics require only momentary attention from the conductor, whereas crescendi and diminuendi require sustained focus.

Sometimes other types of errors are thought by the conductor to be dynamic errors. For example, an intonation error that causes a particular pitch to stand out above the blend (imagine a very flat trumpet pitch) will sound loud to conductors and might be misdiagnosed as a dynamic error. Simply having the player play the note softer seems to make the problem better, but it actually just hides the intonation problem where the volume of the note never was a problem.

Few conductors actually spend time during their score preparation studying the dynamic structure of a work. They rather generally mark some dynamic changes that appear to be important but do not gain an overview of the dynamics of the work in the same way they do the form or phrasing. During score study the conductor should chart the work's dynamic changes the same way the form is charted. This visual aid gives the conductor an overall impression of the dynamic structure of the music. Especially important in contemporary music, this type of score study places an emphasis and focus on dynamic changes that few conductors exercise. Such score study alone will probably improve any conductor's error detection in the area of dynamics.

Another method of improving this kind of error detection is for the conductor to practice expanding his own performance range of dynamics on an instrument. The more the conductor becomes capable and aware of a wide dynamic range, the more he will expect this of other musicians.

As has been repeatedly stated, the conductor should correct errors in balance and blend first, before errors in rhythms and notes. Doing so allows the performers to hear a much different blend in the ensemble. It allows them to tune better to one another and to hear how their rhythmic lines fit into the rhythmic scheme of the work. Doing so allows performers to hear how making the dynamic changes indicated in the score actually affects the sound of the work. Performers find it very frustrating to correctly perform a pianissimo or a long diminuendo only to have it not be heard because it was covered by poor ensemble balance.

ARTICULATION ERRORS

Articulation is one of the most important contributors to musical style. Often the entire character of a work changes simply by playing accents lighter or staccati shorter or sforzandi stronger. Without proper articulation even the correct performance of notes, rhythms, dynamics, and phrasing will be ineffective. This makes articulation errors actually stylistic errors. Unfortunately, many conductors spend very little time on musical style and give little of their energy to correcting articulation errors.

Performers tend to repeat the same articulation errors in all works. Generally speaking, players fall into a comfortable style of articulation and are reluctant to expand their range of articulations. Many performers play most pitches too long. This is a sweeping generalization, but one that is true of ensembles whose conductors are not insistent about musical style. Like the problem of playing everything *mp* or *mf* (mentioned earlier), many players play all pitches with a generic articulation that is not long or short, accented or unaccented, not separated or attached to the notes within the line.

Much music contains three basic articulation markings: the staccato, the slur, and the tenuto. This causes many players to use these three as their only articulation tools. Often the marking (staccacti under slurs) is not played tenuto as intended, but instead as staccato simply because the performer is using one of the three generic articulations and is unfamiliar with this marking. Style sheets might be created by the conductor for each work performed that list the articulation markings and their performance meanings.

A problem for both the performer and conductor is that articulation markings are not absolutes, they are guides. A staccato marking in a work by Stravinsky is a different marking than in a work by Mozart. In order to interpret the markings the performers must be aware of performance practice appropriate to particular composers. Otherwise, the articulation falls back into the generic style again and the overall musical style of the work is lost.

Different instrument characteristics cause performer articulation problems. For example, the slurred line in Example 9-6 is more difficult on a trumpet than it might be on clarinet because on trumpet this is what is called a "lip slur." This means that the player will have to produce the slur by embouchure manipulation, whereas the clarinet easily moves between these notes.

Conductors should learn instrument characteristics in order to predict where articulation problems might occur.

Example 9.6

A common articulation problem is that players tend to extend slurs past their marked ending. The passage in Example 9-7 is a good example. In this exercise many performers will continue the slur across the bar line and not articulate the downbeat pitch.

Example 9.7 Swan Lake, Pyotr Ilyich Tchaikovsky.

Conductors usually hear errors in slurs more easily than accent errors or errors in lengths of pitches. This tendency may be related to the fact that slurring is often associated with melodic phrases. An interruption in the melodic phrase may be easier to detect than other types of errors.

Accent errors seem to be easier to detect than errors in lengths of pitches. This tendency probably is caused by the fact that accents, sforzandi, or fortepiano markings are less common than tenuto, legato, or staccato markings. With fewer of these markings to listen for, the conductor can shift more aural energy to these accents.

Many conductors do not hear errors in lengths of pitches as articulation errors. Often a missed staccato, tenuto, or legato marking is incorrectly identified as a rhythmic problem. This tendency contributes to many inexperienced ensembles playing most music in a connected fashion without accent.

Like players, conductors also often lack the knowledge of performance practice and style required to detect articulation errors. Along with score study, the study of performance practice is, perhaps, the best way to improve articulation in ensembles.

The conductor may also rehearse lines using different articulations from those marked to improve their error-detection skills. This is most helpful during personal practice and can sharpen one's ear to the subtle differences that articulations make in style.

Finally, the conductor must listen to the ends of pitches with as much interest as the beginnings. Most articulations involve the end of a note as much as, if not more than, its beginning. Many articulation errors are errors of the length of pitches.

The exercises in Chapter 10 provide practice for the conductor in detecting each of these primary error types.

CHAPTER 10

Aural Skills Exercises

The musical exercises in this chapter are designed to allow the student conductor to apply skills developed in aural skills courses in a rehearsal setting. The student should prepare the exercise in advance to develop a "correct" version of the exercise as a mental base.

During the class time the instructor should select a piece for performance and ask the student to cover the Error Lists and Explanations of Errors. The instructor should tell the student performers which numbered errors from the Error List should be inserted on each playing. The student conductor will then be required to detect and correct the inserted errors.

The errors have been suggested as the most likely types of errors to occur in each exercise. Explanation of why these errors might occur accompanies each exercise.

RHYTHMIC ERRORS AND ERRORS OF PULSE

Exercise 10.1 ***Ave Verum Corpus,*** Wolfgang Amadeus Mozart

Error List

1. In measure 1, alto move to the D on beat 3 rather than on beat 4.
2. In measure 5 tenor move on beat 3 rather than beat 4.
3. In measure 7 soprano move to the F-sharp on beat 2 rather than on beat 3.
4. All rush beats 1 and 2 of measures 1, 2, and 4.
5. All rush measures 5 and 6 and beats 3 and 4 of measure 7.

Explanation of Errors

Many performers do not actually count long notes or rests but tend to follow the leader. Error 1 occurs when a weaker performer thinks he should have the same rhythm as another performer.

Errors 2 and 3 occur when performers fail to recognize a change in the pattern that has been repeated.

Rushing in slow tempi is much more common than slowing in tempo. This speed up in tempo usually occurs in held pitches.

Slowing in tempo could occur because of error 3. This happens when the pulse unit drags his line.

Exercise 10.2 ***Variations on a Theme by Haydn,*** Johannes Brahms

Error List

1. In measure 5 soprano hold the C on the beat too long and rush the succeeding sixteenth notes.
2. In measure 2 alto read the line as continuing eighth notes rather than quarter notes.
3. In measure 5 bass perform eighth notes as two quarter notes.
4. In measure 3 alto hold quarter note on beat 3 for only an eighth note and move to the next G one eighth note early.
5. Bass perform bars 1 and 2 at twice the speed indicated.
6. Soprano rush bar 4, beat 2.
7. Alto rush beat 1, bar 3 or perform the eighth notes at twice the speed indicated.

Explanation of Errors

Many tempo problems are actually caused by performers confusing the pulse of the work. The speed of this exercise causes many performers to rush rhythms because the quarter note pulse is slow.

Exercise 10.3 ***"Trout" Quintet,*** Franz Schubert

Error List

1. In measure 4 soprano play beat 1 as a dotted eighth/sixteenth rhythm.
2. In bars 7 and 8 tenor play beat 1 as a dotted eighth/sixteenth rhythm.
3. In bar 5 soprano omit the dot and move to the eighth note too early.
4. In bar 4 tenor play beat two as if it was a dotted eighth/sixteenth rhythm.
5. Tenor rush measure 5.
6. Bass move to measure four two counts too early (assumes the conductor is conducting the exercise in four.

Explanation of Errors

Dotted rhythms are often confusing to players, especially those involving thirty-second notes. Often a player mistakes the dotted sixteenth/thirty-second figure for the more common dotted eighth/sixteenth rhythm.

The manner in which a player visualizes a rhythm determines how it is played. The lines in errors 5 and 6 look fast and often are rushed.

Exercise 10.4 ***Sing We and Chant It,*** Thomas Morley

Error List

1. In measure 5 soprano play dotted quarter/eighth rather than the rhythm marked on beat 1.
2. In bar 7 alto hold the tied pitch too long and place the F eighth note on beat two.
3. In bar 4 bass hold the half note for three counts before moving to the quarter note.
4. In measure 5 bass play two eighth notes on count 1 rather than the marked rhythm.
5. All delay beat 3 of measures 2 and 4.
6. Alto drag bars 5–8.
7. Soprano rush bars 1, 2, and 4.

Explanation of Errors

Error 1 is caused by a player reading the rhythm as the same as in measure 3. Tied pitches often cause counting errors such as error 2, and phrase endings give many performers problems in counting.

Error 4 occurs because bass players rarely play complex rhythms and tend to read such rhythms as straight eighth notes.

Many hymnlike excerpts slow in tempo because of unison breathing and phrasing.

Exercise 10.5 *L'Orfeo "Chorus,"* Claudio Monteverdi

Error List

1. In bar 4 bass perform entire line as if in 4/4.
2. In bar 3 soprano double the length of the quarter notes on beat 2.
3. In bar 7 alto perform measure at twice the speed indicated.
4. Alto enter in bar 3 rather than in bar 2.
5. Tenor enter on beat 2 in bar 4 rather than on the "and" of beat 1.
6. Tenor enter in bar 7 rather than bar 4.
7. Soprano rush bar 1.
8. Alto delay entrance of bar 2 slightly and drag bar 3.
9. Soprano and alto accelerate in bars 4, 5, and 6 on the eighth note pattern.

Explanation of Errors

Many pulse errors in 2/2 time can be avoided if players think of the work in the more familiar "cut time." Most errors in 2/2 involve performers doubling the length of pitches and playing as if the meter were 4/4.

Performers often enter slightly late in music of this nature. Tempo is difficult to maintain in imitative music.

Many performers rush repeated rhythmic patterns, especially as they near the end of a phrase.

NOTE ERRORS

Exercise 10.6 *Symphony No. 104, mvt. 1,* Franz Joseph Haydn

Error List

1. In bar 1 soprano perform an F-natural on beat 1 rather than an F-sharp.
2. In bar 1 alto perform a C-natural on beat 4 rather than a C-sharp.
3. In bar 5 soprano perform a C-natural on beat 3 rather than a C-sharp.
4. In bar 7 alto play a C-natural rather than a C-sharp.

Explanation of Errors

All errors in this excerpt are caused by players not reading the key signature.

Exercise 10.7 *"Come Sweet Death,"* J. S. Bach

Error List

1. In bar 3 soprano perform a B-flat rather than a B-natural on the "and" of beat 3.
2. In bar 6 soprano perform an A-natural rather than an A-flat on beat 1.
3. In measure 1 soprano perform a B-natural on beat 2.
4. In measure 5 bass play a B-flat on beat 2 rather than a B-natural.
5. In measure 2 alto play an E-natural rather than an E-flat.

Explanation of Errors

All errors in this exercise are caused by players missing accidentals or not reading the key signature.

Exercise 10.8 ***Serenade, Op. 44, mvt. IV,*** Antonin Dvořák

Error List

1. In bar 5 tenor and bass perform a G-natural rather than a G-sharp.
2. In bars 1 and 3 alto play an A-flat rather than an A-natural.
3. In measure 9 soprano play an F-natural rather than an F-sharp.
4. In measures 9 and 10 bass play B-flats rather than B-naturals.
5. In measures 11 and 12 bass play F-naturals rather than F-sharps.

Explanation of Errors

All errors are caused by performers either missing accidentals or not reading the key signature correctly.

Exercise 10.9 *Slavonic Dances,* Antonin Dvořák

Error List

1. In bars 5, 6, 7, and 8 bass change all Fs to Ds.
2. In bar 1 soprano perform an E-flat on beat 2 rather than a C.
3. In bar 5 tenor perform a C on beat 2 rather than a B-flat.
4. In bars 5, 6, and 7 alto play an F-sharp rather than an F-natural.

Explanation of Errors

Errors 1 and 2 are caused by the players misreading the lines/spaces of their parts. These errors would be most common in brass or vocal groups. Error 3 is caused by a player extending a pattern past its time. Error 4 is caused by players reading this as a D major scale and not remembering the key signature.

Exercise 10.10 *"O Lord Thou God of Truth,"* J. S. Bach

Error List

1. Alto perform F-sharps in measure 1 rather than F-naturals.
2. Alto perform an F-sharp in measure 4 rather than an F-natural.
3. Bass play an E-flat on beat 1 of measure 8.
4. Soprano play a B-natural in bar 4 rather than a B-flat.

Explanation of Errors

Errors 1 and 2 are caused by the player carrying an accidental forward past its time. Error 3 is a missed accidental error. Error 4 is caused by the player not reading the key signature.

INTONATION ERRORS

Exercise 10.11 *Symphony No. 6, mvt. V,* Ludwig van Beethoven

Error List

1. Play the F in bars 1 and 2 flat.
2. Play the As in bar 3 sharp.
3. Play the C in bar 7 and 8 flat.

Explanation of Errors

Errors 1 and 3 are caused by the performer's tendency to expand descending intervals. Error 2 might not need to be added to cause the A in the line to sound out of tune. The M3 of a chord should be adjusted slightly flatter to sound in tune.

Exercise 10.12 *"Come Sweet Death,"* J. S. Bach

Error List

1. Soprano play the Gs in bars 1 and 2 flat.
2. Soprano play the E-flat in bar 5 sharp.

3. Soprano play the E-flat in bars 7 and 8 flat.
4. Soprano play the B in bar 4 sharp.
5. Tenor play the B-flat in measure 2 flat.
6. Tenor play the final G sharp.

Explanation of Errors

Error 1 is caused by the performer hearing the line continuing in descending M2s rather than reading the final interval as the m2. Errors 2 and 3 occur when performers allow the pitch to rise as a melodic line ascends and to go flat as the line descends. Errors 4, 5, and 6 are the natural tendencies of these intervals. Performers need to learn to adjust these intervals as they realize the function of their pitch in the vertical structure.

Exercise 10.13 *Symphony No. 2, mvt. 1,* Johannes Brahms

Error List

1. Soprano play the A in bar 2 sharp.
2. Soprano play the A in bar 3 flat.
3. Alto play the A in bar 2 flat.
4. Bass play the A in bars 2, 3, and 4 flat.

Explanation of Errors

All errors are caused by the performers expanding the intervals. Wide leaps are often expanded, especially when descending, and a high pitch (such as the A in soprano in bar 2) is often played sharp when slurred into.

Exercise 10.14 ***If Thou Be Near,*** J. S. Bach

Error List

1. Soprano play the E-flat in bar 1 sharp.
2. Bass perform the E-naturals in bar 5 sharp.
3. Soprano play the C in bar 7 sharp.
4. Tenor play the D in bar 9 sharp.
5. Alto play the F in bar 9 flat.

Explanation of Errors

Errors 1 and 3 are caused by the performer's tendency to expand wide leaps. Both cause the third of a major chord to be raised too high. Error 2 is caused by the bass not recognizing the E-natural as the root of a diminished seventh chord. The tendency will be to play this pitch sharp because of the ascending line. Errors 4 and 5 are opposite of how these pitches must be adjusted in order to play the chord in tune.

Exercise 10.15 ***Symphony No. 9, mvt. IV,*** Ludwig van Beethoven

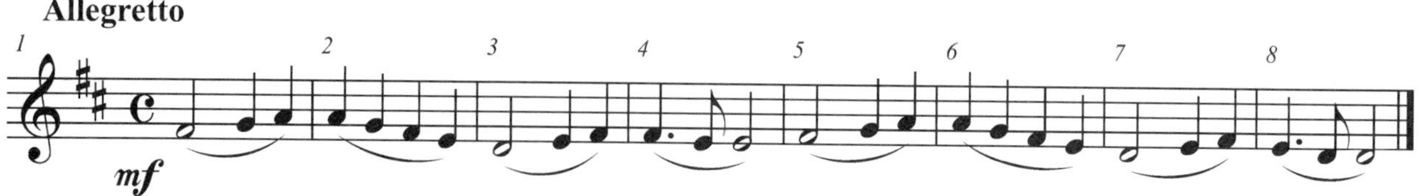

Error List

1. Play the As in bars 1 and 2 flat.
2. Play the F-sharp in bar 4 sharp.
3. Play the F-sharp in bar 6 flat.
4. Play the D in measure 7 flat.

Explanation of Errors

Errors in the intonation of MSs and m2s are difficult to detect. These errors are usually caused by the musician attempting to repeat the interval just performed.

DYNAMIC AND ARTICULATION ERRORS

Exercise 10.16 *A Toye,* Giles Farnabye

Error List

1. Bass perform the entire line *piano.*
2. Soprano perform the entire line *forte.*
3. Tenor and bass play none of the markings.
4. Soprano do not play the accents.

Explanation of Errors

Many ensembles are poorly balanced, usually with the upper parts louder than the lower sounds. Errors 1 and 2 create this "inverted double pyramid" of balance. Error 3 and 4 are also very common. Many players play everything with a generic articulation unless coaxed to do otherwise.

Exercise 10.17 ***Swan Lake,*** Pyotr Ilyich Tchaikovsky

Error List

1. Slur across the bar line into bar 2, connecting the E of bar 1 to the F-sharp of bar 2.
2. Omit all slurs in measure 3.
3. Omit all slurs in bar 6.

Explanation of Errors

Performers relate slurring to phrasing and often continue a slur beyond its marking in order to slur an entire phrase. Errors 2 and 3 are more common in brass than strings or woodwind because downward slurs are often difficult. Players sometimes omit or alter articulations to whatever is easiest on their instrument.

Exercise 10.18 ***Symphony No. 8, mvt. 1,*** Franz Schubert

Error List

1. Tenor slur all of bars 1 and 2 together.
2. Soprano perform all pitches staccato.
3. Tenor omit the crescendo in measures 6–8.
4. Soprano play the entire line *forte.*

Explanation of Errors

Performers, when making slurring errors, usually slur more notes together than indicated. The *portato* marking in the soprano line is unfamiliar to many non–string players and is often misplayed staccato. Without the conductor's insistence, the tenor player might not perform the written crescendo. Soprano line players become accustomed to playing louder dynamics because they usually carry the melody.

Exercise 10.19 ***Quartet, Op. 51, No.2, mvt. IV,*** Johannes Brahms

Error List

1. All omit the accents in bars 4 and 6.
2. Bass and tenor omit the staccato markings throughout.
3. Bass play the entire line *pp.*
4. Soprano play the entire line *forte.*
5. All omit the slur in measure 6.

Explanation of Errors

Many performers do not play articulations at all unless the conductor demands it of them. This would account for errors 1 and 2. As stated before, the balance of many ensembles is top heavy. Errors 3 and 4 will create a strident, bright sound. Error 5 is more common in brass, again, because these types of slurs are not as difficult on string or woodwind instruments.

Exercise 10.20 ***Symphony No. 4, mvt. IV,*** Pyotr Ilyich Tchaikovsky

Error List

1. Soprano omit all staccati in bars 1 and 2.
2. Bass play entire line mp.
3. Soprano omit all slurs.
4. Soprano perform the notes marked with a tenuto as if they were marked staccato.

Explanation of Errors

Errors 1 and 4 are caused by the very common problem of players reading only the notes and rhythms of a line. Error 2 is common because of poor balance. Error 3 might occur because no other notes in the line prior to these were slurred.

ERRORS OF ALL TYPES

Exercise 10.21 ***Symphony No. 29, mvt. 1,*** Wolfgang Amadeus Mozart

Error List

1. Soprano omit accidentals in bars 1 and 3.
2. Bass omit quarter rest in bar 3.
3. Tenor rush eighth note line in bars 1–4.
4. Tenor omit all staccati in bars 1–4.
5. All perform bars 7 and 8 *mp*.
6. All play bars 1–4 *mf*.
7. Bass play the first two bars without any flats.
8. Alto play the E-flats in bars 2 and 4 flat.

Exercise 10.22 ***Symphonie Fantastique,*** Hector Berlioz

Error List

1. Bass play the entire excerpt *mp*.
2. Soprano omit beat 1 of bar 6 (the tied-over F) and move to the D on beat 1, bar 6.
3. Soprano play E-naturals in bars 2 and 3.
4. Alto omit the accents in bars 4, 5, and 6.
5. All omit the decrescendo in bars 7 and 8.
6. Alto play B-naturals in bars 2 and 3.

Exercise 10.23 ***Symphony No. 94, mvt. IV,*** Franz Joseph Haydn

Error List

1. In measure 5 alto hold the tied over G too long and play the remainder of bar 5 and bar 6 on the beat.
2. Soprano rush measures 4, 5, and 6.
3. Alto, tenor, and bass omit crescendo in bars 5 and 6.
4. Alto omit accidentals in bars 1 and 11.
5. Bass play a C-natural rather than a C-sharp in bar 13.
6. Bass and tenor omit slurs in bars 11 and 12.
7. Tenor play entire line *p*.
8. Bass play Ds in m. 8, 9, and 10 flat.

Exercise 10.24 *Symphony No. 6, mvt. II,* Pyotr Ilyich Tchaikovsky

Error List

1. Soprano omit the dot in bars 2 and 4.
2. Bass shorten each of the first 4 measures by one beat of rest, playing each bar in 4/4 rather than 5/4.
3. Soprano omit all crescendi and diminuendi.
4. Tenor play the entire line *pp*.
5. Soprano play F-natural and C-natural in measures 1, 3, and 4.
6. Alto omit accidentals in bars 5 and 7.
7. Bass play upper Ds in bars 1, 3, and 6 flat.
8. Tenor play final note as an A-flat.

Exercise 10.25 ***Water Music "Air,"*** George Frideric Handel

Error List

1. All play the entire excerpt *mp*.
2. Soprano omit all the accents.
3. Bass play B-naturals in bars 1 and 2.
4. Soprano and alto play dotted eighth/sixteenth lines as if written as triplets.
5. Tenor play the first four bars flat.
6. Bass play the final pitch sharp.

Bibliography

Bamberger, Carl. *The Conductor's Art.* McGraw-Hill, New York, 1965.

Barra, Donald. *The Dynamic Performance: A Performer's Guide to Musical Expression and Interpretation.* Prentice Hall, Englewood Cliffs, NJ, 1983.

Battisti, Frank and Robert Garofalo. *Guide to Score Study for Wind Band Conductors.* Meredith Music Publications, Ft. Lauderdale, FL, 1990.

_____ *The Winds of Change.* Meredith Music, Galesville, MD, 2002.

Berlioz, Hector. *The Orchestral Conductor.* Carl Fischer, New York, 1923.

Berry, Wallace. *Form in Music (2nd ed.).* Prentice Hall, Englewood Cliffs, NJ, 1986.

Demaree, Robert W. Jr. and Don V. Moses. *The Complete Conductor.* Prentice Hall, Englewood Cliffs, NJ, 1995.

Garofalo, Robert. *Guides to Band Masterworks.* Meredith Music, Ft. Lauderdale, FL, 1992.

______ *Improving Intonation in Band and Orchestra Performance.* Meredith Music, Ft. Lauderdale, FL, 1996.

Goldman, Richard Franko. *The Concert Band.* Rinehart and Co., New York, 1946.

____ *The Wind Band: Its Literature and Technique.* Allyn & Bacon, Boston, 1962.

Green, Elizabeth and Nicolai Malko. *The Conductor's Score.* Prentice Hall, Englewood Cliffs, NJ, 1985.

____ and Mark Gibson. *The Modern Conductor (7th ed.).* Pearson Prentice Hall, Upper Saddle River, NJ, 2004.

Harris, Jr., Frederick. *Conducting with Feeling.* Meredith Music, Galesville, MD, 2001.

Hunsberger, Donald and Roy Ernst. *The Art of Conducting (2nd ed.).* McGraw-Hill, New York, 1992.

Jacobson, Bernard. *Conductors on Conducting.* Columbia Publishing Co., Inc., Frenchtown, NJ, 1979.

Kohut, Daniel and Joe W. Grant. *Learning to Conduct and Rehearse.* Prentice Hall, Englewood Cliffs, NJ, 1990.

Labuta, Joseph. *Basic Conducting Techniques (2nd. ed.).* Prentice Hall, Englewood Cliffs, NJ, 1989.

Lebrecht, Norman. *The Maestro Myth.* Birch Lane Press, New York, 1991.

Leinsdorf, Erich. *The Composer's Advocate.* Yale University Press, New Haven, 1981.

Maiello, Anthony. *Conducting: A Hands-on Approach.* Warner Bros. Pubs., Miami, FL, 1996.

Malko, Nicolai. *The Conductor and His Baton.* Wilhelm Hansen, Copenhagen, 1950.

McBeth, Francis. *Effective Performance of Band Music.* Southern Music, San Antonio, TX, 1972.

Prausnitz, Frederick. *Score and Podium: A Complete Guide to Conducting.* W.W. Norton, New York, 1983.

Rudolf, Max. *The Grammar of Conducting.* G. Schirmer, New York, 1980.

Saito, Hideo. *The Saito Conducting Method.* Ongaku No Tomo Sha Corp., Tokyo, Japan, 1956. Translated version by Fumihiko Torigai (ed. Wayne J. Toews), Tokyo, 1988.

Scherchen, Herman. *Handbook of Conducting (3rd ed.).* DaCapo, Garden City, NY, 1978.

Schonberg, Harold C. *The Great Conductors.* Simon & Schuster, New York, 1967.

Schuller, Gunther. *The Compleat Conductor.* Oxford University Press, New York, 1997.

Wagar, Jeannine. *Conductors in Conversations.* G.K. Hall & Co., Boston, 1995.

Wagner, Richard. *On Conducting.* Dover Publications, Mineola, N.Y., 1989.

Walter, Bruno. *Of Music and Music Making.* Norton, New York, 1961.

Weingartner, Felix. *On Conducting.* Kalmus, n.d., New York.

Whitwell, David. *The Art of Musical Conducting.* WINDS, Northridge, CA, 1998.

Musical Examples Index

Subject Index